ENDORSEMENTS

Charles Whitfield takes us into the heart and soul of *A Course in Miracles*. This book summarizes and clarifies it. It is an excellent companion to reading the Course itself. ...Highly recommended.

Jyoti and Russell Park, PhD
Center for Sacred Studies, California

This book takes over where the Twelve Steps leave off. Charles Whitfield skillfully explains the connections between the Twelve Steps and the spirituality of *A Course in Miracles* and the growth we can have beyond Twelve Step work.

Jack C., Twelve Step Fellowship Member

A Course in Miracles comes from the same intelligence that we visited in our Near-death experience.
This book clearly summarizes much of that spiritual wisdom.

Jane S., Near-death experiencer

I had heard of *A Course in Miracles* but never made time to read it. I eventually got a copy of it and started reading but couldn't get into it. This book helped me finally open it again, and even more, to understand many of its main and powerful messages.

Stephen Mitchell, Fine Arts Director, Private School

COVER PICTURE

In 1975 I painted this whimsical representation in oils after having begun to meditate daily for two years. For the prior ten years I had been a staunch atheist. I was also beginning to learn about and study the Twelve Steps and was perhaps the first physician faculty member teaching in a medical school to require all medical students to attend an AA meeting. Little did I know that when I painted this picture that it would be so appropriate for the cover of this book. When I read in the Course about the real meaning of the Lion and Lamb metaphor I reviewed what had evolved for me psychologically and spiritually over the next few years wherein I continued to meditate daily and about 1977 began reading *A Course in Miracles*. Over the years I have referred to the Course countless times in the numerous talks I gave about trauma, addictions, and the recovery process.

The cover of my first book on the Course titled *Choosing God* shows a painting on an antique stained glass window of a white dove, which is a symbol of the Holy Spirit.

On the cover of this book *Teachers of God* that you hold in your hands is another spiritual symbol tied to the Course, the Lion and the Lamb lying beside one another, with the Lion as strength and the Lamb as vulnerability and innocence. The Course mentions other spiritual symbols which I summarize on page 90 of *Choosing God* (which is volume one of this two volume pair of books on the Course's main teachings.) I also painted the Lamb here as being translucent, adding another dimension to this Lamb as a Christ figure, in part since Jesus was described as looking semi-transparent in *The Urantia Book* (e.g., its pages 2029 and 2055) of how he appeared to the apostles after the resurrection.

TEACHERS OF GOD

Further Reflections on A Course in Miracles

FOR — SPIRITUAL SEEKERS,

PEOPLE IN RECOVERY,

THOSE IN TWELVE STEP FELLOWSHIPS,

NEAR-DEATH EXPERIENCERS,

AGNOSTICS, ATHEISTS,

AND

THE RELIGIOUSLY AND SPIRITUALLY CURIOUS

Charles L Whitfield, MD

Author of *Healing The Child Within* and *The Power of Humility*

ꟿꝮP

muse house press

Muse House Press

ISBN: 978-1-935827-01-6

Trade Paperback

Copyright © 2010 Charles L. Whitfield

All Rights Reserved

Requests for information and rights should be addressed to:
Muse House Press
Find us on the Internet at:

www.MuseHousePress.com

www.cbwhit.com

www.BarbaraWhitfield.com

Muse House Press and the MHP Logo are imprints of Muse House Press.

Cover design and Interior composition by:

Donald Brennan / YakRider Media

Printed in the United States of America

Second Printing

ACKNOWLEDGMENTS

Grateful thanks and acknowledgment for permission to use or quote material from the following sources:

To Kenneth Wapnick for his several identified quotes and for permission to reproduce his Chart 1 from his 1990 book *A Vast Illusion*: Time according to ACIM.

To Robert Perry for permission for me to summarize some of his work on the Course, including his review of the evolution of the Course versions in a scholarly article on his website: www.circleofa.org.

To Allen Watson for permission to reproduce his Chart of The Journey Home from his 1994 book *The Journey Home*.

To my wife Barbara for her help typing the manuscript and our ongoing studying the Course together and individually.

To Donald Brennan for his excellent layout and graphic design of this book.

To my many other colleagues, some cited in the references here, who write and teach about the Course for their continued inspiration, and to the members of the Board of the Foundation for Inner Peace for their unselfish giving of the Course to us.

To Alcoholics Anonymous for permission to reproduce its Twelve Steps

And to Helen Schucman and Bill Thetford for receiving *A Course in Miracles* and sharing it with us all with the editorial assistance of Kenneth Wapnick and the publishing assistance of Judy Skutch Whitson of the Foundation for Inner Peace; and to the latter two fo r permission to reproduce photos from the archives of ACIM and the DVD Memories of Helen & Bill.

DEDICATION

FOR — SPIRITUAL SEEKERS,

PEOPLE IN RECOVERY,

THOSE IN TWELVE STEP FELLOWSHIPS,

NEAR-DEATH EXPERIENCERS,

AGNOSTICS, ATHEISTS,

AND

THE RELIGIOUSLY AND SPIRITUALLY CURIOUS

Table of Contents

TABLES

FIGURES

USING REFERENCES TO THE COURSE IN
This Book

I use a more reader-friendly reference method than most writers on the Course. For example, for a quote's reference code of **67T, 1:6**

- the **67** denotes the **page number** in the Course,

T indicates that it is in the **Text** volume of the Course,

1 means the **paragraph on that page,** and

6 means the **sentence** of that paragraph, as numbered in the recent editions of ACIM.

I list three more supplemtal books below the standard three.

T = Text

W = Workbook,

M = Manual for Teachers,

P = Psychotherapy,

S = Song of Prayer,

C = Clarification of Terms (at end of Manual for Teachers)

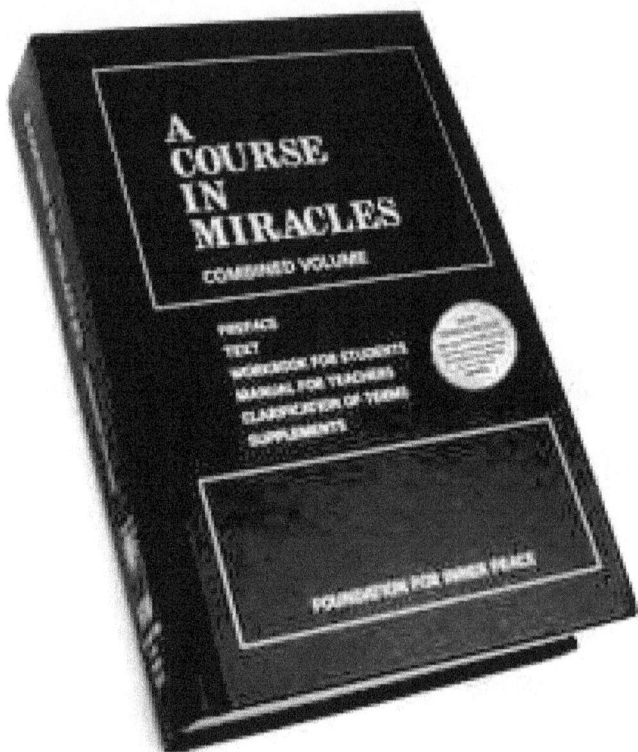

PREFACE

A Course in Miracles is the most spiritually exciting book I have ever read. I have found no other spiritual writing as intellectually stimulating, yet so practical in our relationships with ourself, others and God.

Do you want peace or pain? If you want peace, the Course suggests, "Choose God." It's that simple. What is not so simple is knowing exactly why, when and how to choose God. The Course provides answer after answer to these questions and more. And it gives us ongoing psychological nourishment.

A major focus of the Course is on the process of forgiveness by letting go of our ego. But over the last century the ego has been more misunderstood than clear. The Course makes our understanding of the ego as clear as I have ever seen it, which makes it easier to let it go.

People in the forefront of psychology and relationships have long realized the need for a bridge between psychology and spirituality. The Course provides that bridge. As a physician and therapist I have long observed my patients getting better by adding spirituality to their program of recovery. I have also seen numerous people in Twelve Step programs use the Course to expand and continue their Twelve Step work.

I have used the Course personally as spiritual nourishment for over 30 years, and it has enriched all of my relationships. For eight years, my wife Barbara and I read a section from it to one another most mornings after breakfast. We have also taught its principles together. I especially like that the Course is a private and personal exchange between me and its author. There is no other authority figure imposing itself between me and what he is saying.

NEW FOR THIS VOLUME

This book is a continuation of volume 1 – *Choosing God*: A Birds-Eye View of *A Course in Miracles,* of this two volume pair. That book starts slowly and gradually builds to provide a basic explanation for its major teachings. In that book I introduced how the Course was related to the Bible, the Twelve Steps of Alcoholics Anonymous and other fellowships, and the process or recovery from illness. I have also used it in the classes I teach on spirituality in general and on the Course in particular here in Atlanta and across the country, including at the Rutgers University Summer School of Alcohol and Drug Studies over a 25-year span .

To make this second volume -- *Teachers of God* -- that you hold in your hands more understandable and enjoyable to read, I suggest that you consider reading *Choosing God* first, especially if you are not already familiar with many of the basic principles of the Course.

If you are **already substantially familiar with the Course**, this book may now give you more understanding of the rich psycho-spiritual nourishment that the Course offers.

While it may provide a clear and useful overview of its major teachings, this book is **not** intended to be **a substitute for reading and studying the Course**. To get its full meaning and message, I recommend that anyone stimulated by this or any other book that addresses it get a copy of the Course and read it regularly. There is no substitute for the real words.

And in this book I include in the Appendix a new and previously unpublished article on the relationship of the Course with other faiths and Twelve Step fellowships titled The Universal Message of the Course (see page 121).

With that said, I hope that this book *Teachers of God*, will provide a useful guide to understanding the powerful and yet peaceful message of *A Course in Miracles.*

1 THE DREAMER AND THE DREAM

"You travel but in dreams, while safe at home." (257T, 17:7)

Who is the dreamer? And what is the dream? The Course says that *we* are the dreamer. But the dream itself is more complicated. The Course's description of the dream reminds me of what others have said about our "cosmic story," the Hindu spiritual story "Lila," or the mythological Hero's Journey or adventure that to me is part of the Divine Mystery.

The Course says that prior to our earthly incarnation, we were aware of our perfect Oneness in God, and knew that there was nothing else, either outside or inside this Oneness. (359T) Then we thought of the notion ("the tiny, mad idea") that we were somehow separate from God's Oneness and that we could even take God's place -- and at that insane idea, we forgot to laugh. (544T) At that moment we made time and several other characteristics of the ego, as shown in the upper half of Figure 1.

The Course says that based on the above, in our resulting and continuing "separated" state we are asleep, as though we are in a dream. Yet, it says, "You dwell not here, but in eternity. You travel but in dreams, while safe at home."(275T, 6-7) In his comprehensive 1990 book on the Course and time, *A Vast Illusion*, Ken Wapnick, from his detailed understanding of the Course, says that *in the "reality" of the illusion/dream, the entire scope of the past billions of years happened in one short instant*. In this short instant *two scripts* happened: **we made our ego** and all of its characteristics and effects (see top half of figure1) and **God** instantly **gave us** the **Holy Spirit** which corrected the ego separation and all its seeming effects.

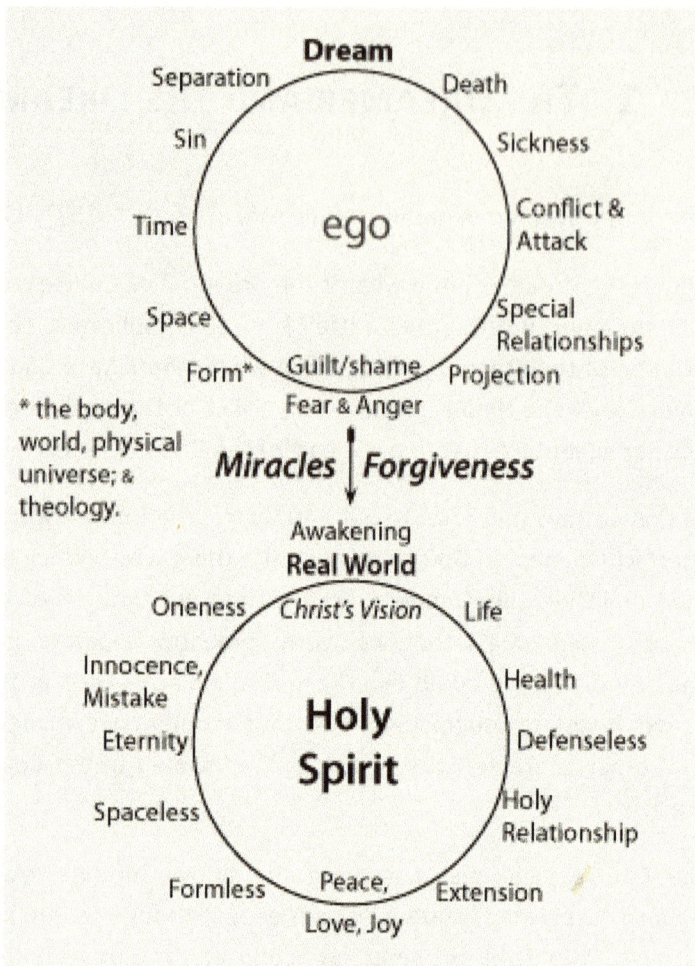

Figure 1.
The Holy Spirit corrects the ego's Dream/Nightmare Back toward Our Original: the Real World and Christ's Vision

The Course says that these are our *only* two scripts: the ego's dream/nightmare and the Holy Spirit's gentle and loving correction. This leaves us with a constant choice at any moment for being in either one. As outlined in *Choosing God* (and described in detail in the Course), the part of us that makes that choice is in our mind (where everything else happens as well), and that we can call it the *decision maker, choice maker,* and *observer,* in part similar to the "observer self" described by psychoanalyst Arthur Deikman in his 1982 book *The Observing Self.* In fact, *we* wrote the ego script *as* decision-/choice-maker/observer and are also our script's producer, director, actors, and audience—a scenario that many spiritual masters and writers have noted.

... And if we wrote it, we can erase it.

THE DREAM IN TIME

What comes next is difficult for me to understand. It is related to the Course's concept of time, which I describe more in the next two chapters. The Course says that as we appear to be experiencing things now, we are actually *re*-experiencing them. This is because everything – including the "separation" (also called the "fall") and God's correction for it -- has *already happened.* Today, in time, we simply project what we believe, think and feel onto the screen of our life, and that is what we experience. As Wapnick interprets the Course, "...we are observing what has already happened, and ...what appear to us to be distinct events taking place in a linear progression of past, present, and future are rather all present simultaneously in our minds because the whole of time occurred in one single instant. We focus directly only on segments of the total fragmentation at any given moment, and choose whether to view the ego's version of separation, attack, anger, and specialness, or the Holy Spirit's correction of all this through [miracles], forgiveness, and holy relationships." (Wapnick 1990)

When we remember that we have chosen what we are experiencing, the chains that seemingly bind us to our "observing chair" and the "screen" of our life onto which we project our choices fall away, and the screen disappears, and we are free (Wapnick 1990). As we awaken, we are now free to choose *when* we will review *what,* while our life unfolds. As a part of the Divine Mystery, we make these things happen in large part each time that we choose God or our ego.

3

As we dream, we are reliving the initial separation into all our relationships. Our reliving of the separation can then activate within us a **reverberation of the original** guilt, shame and fear that we felt when we thought we left God. Our only job now is to *un*do our ego script in our dream of separation, as summarized at the top of figure 1.We do that, or rather undo it, each time that we choose God over our ego.

As we continue to co-create miracles, we will know that we are on the path of doing our only job -- realizing the Atonement. At the same time, however, we can remember that the undoing of the ego, and the Atonement itself, have already been accomplished. This is because at the same instant that we thought we separated from God, God created the Holy Spirit, and thereby extended Himself directly into our illusory script-dream.

A COLLECTIVE RELIGIOUS DREAM?

Some of this information that the Course gives us may clash with our prior religious experience. And it will certainly clash with our ego's ideas, as shown in Table 1. We could even view these as being a kind of collective religious dream. This is because both the ego and our traditional Judeo-Christian religious training and experience say that we left God and are sinners who deserve to be punished. The ego adds that through our attachment to the ego we also tried to take over God's role. In summary, conventional Judeo-Christian religion says, in part, that we are separated from others and God, and are sinners − suffering and unsafe.

By contrast, the Course says that we neither left God nor tried to take God's place, that we are not sinners, and that God loves us unconditionally and will never punish us. This kind of spiritual information is essentially the opposite of many of our prior Western religious assumptions, and it may upset us, especially on an ego level. But somewhere deep in our hearts we may have a memory, no matter how faint, that we are one with others in God, perfect, eternal, unchangeable

4

and safe. In one of its more beautiful sections, the Course describes such a memory:

"Listen, -- perhaps you catch a hint of an ancient state not quite forgotten; dim, perhaps, and yet not altogether unfamiliar, like a song whose name is long forgotten, and the circumstances in which you heard completely unremembered. Not the whole song has stayed with you, but just a little wisp of melody, attached not to a person or a place or anything particular. But you remember, from just this little part, how lovely was the song..." (446T, 6:1-3)

"Bad" Dreams

Just as there are often subplots, or dreams-within-a-dream in our ordinary sleep experience, the Course describes a range of painful dreams within our ego's overall dream of separation. These sub-dreams span from general *suffering*, when we focus on all that the world has done to injure us (581T, 12:1-3), to a kind of *nightmare*, wherein we dream that others are out to get us, and/or that we are out to get them (584T, 12: 1-3). We believe that others do to us exactly what we unconsciously think that we did to them. Once we are so deluded into blaming them, we don't see the actual *cause* of what we or they do, because we want them to be guilty. And the Course says, the cause is in our own mind, from which we project our own pain onto others. Where our pain begins, it can here and now end.

Question or Tenet	ego / Religion	A Course in Miracles
Did we leave God?	Yes. (The "fall.")	No. We never left God.
Did we try to usurp God?	Yes	No. We are part of God.
Are we sinners?	Yes	No.
God's response	Punish us	Loves us unconditionally.
Summary	We are separated from others & God, unsafe and suffering *	We are one with God, perfect, eternal, unchangeable and safe.

Table 1.
Major Tenets of ego and Religion
Contrasted with the Course's

*The Judeo-Christian and Catholic religions and their many denominations do offer a way out, although most focus on the information in the middle column, e.g., we must first admit/confess our sins, sacrifice, and ask God's forgiveness, with Judaism perhaps leaning less in that direction.

In our mind, our decision-, or choice-maker made up the ego's dream world when we chose the ego over God. It left us with the dream, which, as shown in figure 1, includes: separation, sin, time, space, form, emotional pain, projection, special relationships, conflict and attack, sickness and death, as shown in the upper half of Figure 1. The Course describes our bad dream further:

It is "A timelessness in which time is made real; a part of God that can attack itself; a separate brother as enemy; a mind within a body, all are forms of circularity whose ending starts at its beginning, ending at its cause. The world you see depicts exactly what you thought you did. Except that now you think that what you did is being done to you. ... It [the guilty world you project] keeps you narrowly confined within a body, which it punishes because of all the sinful things the body does within its dream." (587T, 7 :1-6)

AWAKENING

Is there a way out of our painful dream? The Course says "yes" many times, e.g., :

➤ "The secret of salvation is but this: that you are doing this unto yourself. No matter what the form of the attack, this still is true. ... Whatever seems to be the cause of any pain and suffering you feel, this is still true. For you would not react at all to figures in a dream you knew that you were dreaming. Let them be as hateful and as vicious as they may, they could have no effect on you unless you failed to recognize it as your dream.' (587T, 10:1-6)

➤ "This single lesson learned will set you free from suffering, whatever form it takes. ... [The Holy Spirit] would teach you but the single cause of all [your pain].... . And you will understand that miracles reflect the simple statement, 'I have done this thing, and it is this I would undo.' " (588T, 11:1-6) (These important quotes are repeated in part later)

7

This idea of our ultimately being *responsible* for our own *unnecessary pain* is said elsewhere in the Text:

➢ "I am responsible for what I see. I choose the feelings I experience, and I decide upon the goal I would achieve. And everything that seems to happen to me I ask for, and receive as I have asked." (448T, 2:3-5)

By practicing miracles, we can begin to let go of our attachment to our ego and its dream world. By so turning our life over to the *care* of God, as the third of the Twelve Steps addresses, we can begin to let go of our pain, and eventually even forgive ourself for our mistakes. By this process, we awaken to seeing the real world, with Christ's vision, which is the goal of the Course. As shown in the bottom half of Figure 1 above, we can now experience our original Being in God's real world, including: Oneness, innocence, eternity, spacelessness, timelessness, peace, love and joy, extension, holy relationships, defenselessness, health and a peaceful life.

Although we forgot, we are innocent children of God, and unknowingly we caused our own pain. By co-creating miracles we can now awaken and realize that our painful melodrama is all a dream.

The introduction to the Course says:

Nothing real can be threatened.

Nothing unreal exists

Herein lies the peace of God.

As we progressively awaken, we can realize what is real: God and God's real world. We do so by removing the blocks to our ability to see with Christ's vision, i.e., our "awareness of love's presence." These blocks are our attachment to the ego and its dream world.

We awaken into what the Course calls the forgiving or happy dream, which we experience when we co-create miracles and let go of our attachment to our ego. Here we can summarize: the Course says that the ego's dream is a nightmare, and that it is neither lasting nor real. By contrast, the real world is 1) when we awaken to being in the world but not in it, 2) similar to "lucid dreaming," 3) practicing miracles and forgiveness (letting go and letting God), and thereby 4) accepting the Atonement for ourself, which is our only task.

Bill Thetford in California

...when after reading and studying the Course for years
realized that he got it (fully understood it)
and was now free and at peace in God's World.
(In this picture Bill was not at a religious revival meeting.)

2 TIME

The way we experience and view the passage of time may be a factor in how we perceive it. As we have aged, others and I experience time as passing progressively faster -- seemingly increasing in its speed year by year. By contrast, we may experience that time passes more slowly 1) if we are young, 2) in physical or emotional pain or 3) when we are in the flow state. Experiencing time is part of the curicuum and classroom wherein we awaken, learn, evolve and grow. Allen Watson and Ken Wapnick note that "Time can release as well as imprison, depending on whose interpretation of it you use" (13T, 4:1; also 11T, 8:5). Time has several interesting and useful characteristics, according to the Course. Like the body, the world and the physical universe, time is neutral. That neutrality depends on how we see and use it.

The ego and the Holy Spirit have different ideas of what time is for. Let's contrast the Course's two different views.

If we use time according to our ego, which is the way most of us have come to understand and use it, it imprisons and causes us pain. But if we enlist the help of the Holy Spirit in the way we approach time, we can experience peace, and at times even joy.

In Table 2 on the next two pages, I list 12 characteristics of time and summarize how the Course describes the way the Holy Spirit and the ego each view and use it. You may want to read over the table first, and then the text below, or vice versa, to begin slowly to digest this somewhat complex area of the Course.

The Holy Spirit uses time for healing, which releases us from the pain of being time-bound. It does so by undoing our attachment to our ego, which we initiate each time that we co-create a miracle. Accomplished only in the present moment (holy instant), healing saves us time by releasing us from the guilt and shame of the past and fear of the future. (I describe more on healing in the next chapter.)

Characteristic	Holy Spirit	ego
Use	**Healing:** undo ego's world. A teaching/learning device to heal the separation. Uses it without believing in it.	Uses time, space, & the physical to deny our eternal spirit. Destructive, attacking, with pain[1]
Purpose	Undo ego's belief in separation & sin, making the need for time unnecessary: forgiveness/letting go.	Guilt/shame of the past (belief in sin) and fear of punishment in future dominate the present.
Function	Healing in the present; temporary.	Extend time over eternity.
Emphasis	Eternal Now (holy instant) – which is all It knows [2].	Past (guilt & shame) & Future (fear)–all it knows.
Duration	Eternal	Time-bound

Table 2. The Two Uses of Time according to ACIM

---

[1] Our ego makes guilt/shame & fear by believing in sin of the past, projecting it as fear of the future (that God will punish us), thus avoiding the present.

[2] Time has no power over eternity; learning this is time's only purpose for us.

	Holy Spirit	*ego*
Result	Releases us from time.	Keeps us in time to support its painful plan.
Goal	Life and Heaven.	Death and hell.
Our Identity	An eternal part of God.	A body bound by space and time.
The past	Has no [lasting] effects on us.	Caused the present.
Our sins against God	Never happened.	Real.
Use of memory	To focus on present.	To focus on past & future.
God's teachers, miracles & forgiveness	Saves and ends time.	Unaware of these; prolongs time.

Table 2. ... concluded

The Two Uses of Time according to ACIM

The Course also says that, "No one... could ever doubt the power of your learning skill. There is no greater power in the world." (465T, 3:1-2) So, what is it that we might learn here about time? While the Course describes many helpful things to learn, one of the most useful is how to recognize the ego in its various guises, including how it uses time.

The ego uses time to deny and attack our eternal and invulnerable Oneness with God. It does so by constructing a world of separation, sin, time, space, form, guilt, fear, special relationships, sickness and death.

The ego begins with a belief in sin, guilt and fear. Then it makes up a world of time and space to reinforce that belief. It is thus our belief in sin and feeling guilt that is the glue that holds the ego's idea and dream together (Wapnick 1990).

Perhaps in order to survive in a mostly ego-oriented society and world, we at first unknowingly buy into the ego's insane plan, and try to make it work for us. But it doesn't work. It doesn't bring us fulfillment and peace. In fact, following our ego brings us mostly emptiness and pain.

Enter the Course, which offers us a "better way." It suggests that all we have to do is change our mind. We change the way we look at and see things – our *perception*. It says, "This is not a course in philosophical speculation, nor is it concerned with precise terminology. It is concerned only with Atonement, or the correction of perception." (77M, 1:1-2)

By co-creating miracles with God/Holy Spirit/Christ, we change our perception. This shift in perception, which is one of the definitions of a miracle, saves us time by letting us move out of time and up into the Eternal Now, which is the holy instant and where we are always. Figure 2 shows how originally and always we are a part of God, in what the Course calls the "vertical perception," or right-mindedness. (8T, 6:3-5) It thus emphasizes our unity with God, or the Atonement.

Miracle principle 15 addresses its purpose:

"The purpose of time is to enable you to learn to use time constructively. It is thus a teaching device and a means to an end. Time will cease when it is no longer useful in facilitating learning." (4T.15:2-4).

Time:
Now and Here
v.
Then and There
A Course in Miracles

Vertical — true perception — **Holy Instant**
Right mind → **Choose God Now** → Peace/Miracle
No past or future...No sin, guilt, fear

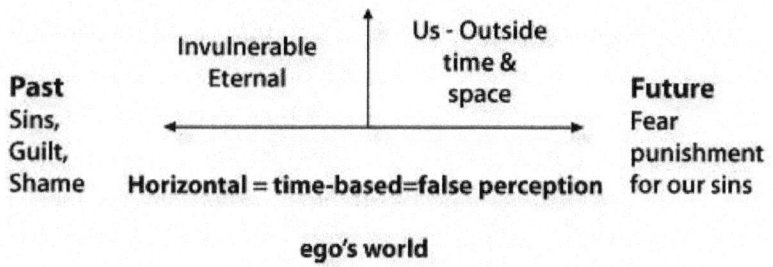

	Invulnerable Eternal	Us - Outside time & space	
Past			**Future**
Sins,			Fear
Guilt,			punishment
Shame	Horizontal = time-based=false perception		for our sins

ego's world

Miracle → *shortens/eliminates time in Atonement*

Figure 2.
Time - Now & Here v. Then & There from ACIM

If we are *in* time, when we identify with the ego and its world, we live in the "horizontal perception" or our conventional conception of time. We are all more than familiar with this thinking and experiencing of time, which includes a past--with its supposed "sins" and their resulting guilt and shame, and a future, with fear of punishment for those sins.

The Course says that by experiencing a miracle we shift from the horizontal (or false) to the vertical (or true perception), or shifting from being time-bound into the holy instant where we feel peace. This is because *Now* has no sin, guilt, shame or fear, because it has no past or future.

By experiencing a miracle, we shorten time, because we are now closer to, or *in* the Atonement. In Chapter 1 of the Text, the miracle principle 47 says: "The miracle is a learning device that lessens the need for time. It establishes an out-of-pattern time interval not under the usual laws of time. In this sense it is timeless." In the next principle (number 48) it adds, "The miracle is the only device at your immediate disposal for controlling time."

The entire vertical axis of Figure 2 - God, Christ, us now, Holy Spirit, holy instant, atonement, miracle, forgiveness, salvation, and true perception (which is Christ's vision), is eternal and invulnerable, and is *outside* of *time* and *space*. It is God and God's world, of which we are each a crucial part.

As part of what I call the "Divine Mystery," we enter into this earthly incarnation that includes ordinary time, space and physical matter—all of which are neutral, although ultimately illusory. We can thus use any of these as we *explore the Mystery*, or what the Course would call "*learn the curriculum*." One important message that we can learn concerns the *resurrection* and its relationship to time. The Course says that our *awakening* from the *ego's dream of death* is the deeper meaning of the resurrection. Although our awakening has already happened and only awaits our acceptance, we can use time to remember this Truth, and be as God created us.

HEALING AND TIME

In my career as a physician and therapist for the past 40-plus years, I have assisted many people as they worked to heal their hurt and pain. The Course's words above and just below fit with much of my experience, both professionally and personally. For example, about healing and time it says "Healing cannot be accomplished in the past. It must be accomplished in the present to release the future." (247T, 9:3-4) The way I have assisted countless people as they heal is to bring their *past* ungrieved pain *into* the *present,* make their experience as real as they can as they *grieve it,* and then *release it* in their own way and time. Sharing it with safe people (described in *A Gift to Myself*) and then turning it over to God is one effective way that I have seen people use to finally release their previously stuck and ungrieved pain. A problem is that to so metabolize significant trauma effects we usually need to tell our story and so grieve numerous times over the time span of countless holy instants.

The Course says that healing, like everything else, happens in our mind. In our mind we are the experiencer, observer and choice-maker. Minute to minute and even second to second, we make the choice to heal, or not. Healing is facilitated any time two people join together in a desire to help and be helped – as Bill Thetford and Helen Schucman did as they committed to finding "a better way" to handling their conflicts in 1965. And as Bill Wilson and Dr. Bob Smith did in founding Alcoholics Anonymous in 1935. And as countless others do in Twelve Step fellowships daily, and those in group and individual therapy do regularly today. In the supplement booklet "Psychotherapy" - an extended part of the Course, it says, "Healing is limited by the limitations of the psychotherapist, as it is limited by the patient. The aim of the process, therefore, is to transcend these limits. ... One asks for help; another hears and tries to answer in the form of help. This is the formula for salvation, and must heal." (7 P)

Wapnick (1990) suggests further that other spiritual paths that operate within a linear time frame may work if their goal is God. But, he says, they will take a much longer period of time because of the reality accorded to the ego's temporal tricks. In my view from studying the Course, these tricks may be the ego's misuse of time to support its belief in sin, guilt/shame and fear, as show in the overview Table 3. This can end up imprisoning or binding us in time. By contrast, the Holy Spirit corrects and releases us from the ego's insane idea of separating from God and trying to take God's place. It does so by showing us that not only is there no past sin, therefore no present guilt and shame, and no fear of God's punishment in the future, but that when we are in the holy instant there is no time either.

Time according to -	Action	Past	Present	Future
ego	Imprisons us in time	Sees only sin	We feel guilt & shame	We fear punishment for our "sins"
Holy Spirit	Corrects & releases us from being stuck in time	Knows no sin	No use for guilt or shame	No use for fear -- we are invulnerable and safe in God)

Table 3.
An Overview of Time according to ACIM

18

An Experience Without Time

The following is from a student of the Course who had a near-death experience prior to finding the Course.

"After severe back surgery I started to die. I lost consciousness and awoke in what I could later call a "Tunnel." At the time this happened I had no words for It. My grandmother who had been dead for 14 years put her arms around me and I felt all the toxic pain (ego) I had carried in this lifetime fall away. After a while I started moving away from her. But I felt at peace with that because I knew she would always be there waiting for me. Later, this incredible energy that I believe to be God held me and we reviewed my life. I could feel what everyone else in my life could feel because of my actions. I could feel all the love I had given and I could feel the pain I was responsible for, too. When there was pain, God held me even tighter so I could withstand it. My 32 year life passed by me in a linear fashion, and nothing was omitted. The doctors told me that I was out for 20 minutes, but I felt like I relived 32 years.

"I have been back in this reality for 33 years now. Time has never been the same. I feel like there is no time. We are here in eternity. To me, it is only our bodies that need time to function. The real me is eternal and all of our world is eternal. Time is an illusion. When I feel 'time' I am in my ego. When there is 'no time' I feel I am home, here."

The Course says that: We are observing and experiencing what has already happened in linear time of past, present and future. We focus on segments, in time, and choose, consciously or not, God or ego. We are responsible for what and when we choose.

I will continue this bird's-eye-view of time from the Course in the next chapter.

This instant is the only time there is.

A Course in Miracles p 443

---

3 SAVING TIME

The Course says that practicing miracles saves us time. For example, when we co-create a miracle, we *heal a conflict*, thereby lessening our need for any additional time that it may take to heal that conflict, with all its mental, emotional, and physical pain. While miracles occur in time, they also "collapse" it, and thereby saving us time.

Over time, by practicing a string of cumulative miracles, the time that we save adds up to a sizeable number of years. "Here is the quick and open door through which you slip past centuries of effort, and escape from time." (390T, 7:3) Wapnick says, "We skip over the 'thousand years' it would have taken us to let go of our grievances of being unfairly treated." Of course, we save this time only from a level two perspective, since in level one we discover that time as horizontal past-present-future does not exist, as shown in table 4.

Level 1	It has all happened already. There is no time.
Level 2	We heal, or not - using time - by *letting go* of ego, past & future.

Table 4.
Time According to Two Levels of Understanding

The string of miracles leads to forgiveness, which saves us more time being stuck in the ego's pain. And both of these lead to holy relationships, which save still more time. Finally, the Course says that being an aware teacher of God also saves us time. (I address the characteristics of a Teacher of God in Chapter 8 below.)

Our being in a holy relationship saves us time. By seeing our own ego/guilt/shame in others, and which we have projected onto them, we can begin to let go of these toxic and painful experiences by practicing miracles and forgiveness. The Course says, "You have no idea of the tremendous release and deep peace that comes from meeting yourself and your brothers totally without judgment. ... judging... in any way is without meaning." (47T, 3:1-2)

Now, without judgment, in the holy relationship with our brother or sister time stops for us both *in* and *as* the holy instant. The Course says, "Here is the ultimate release which everyone will find in his own way, at his own time. ...Time has been saved for you because you and your brother are together. This is the special means this Course is using to save you time." (389T, 6:1-4) (See also Chapter 14 below and *Choosing God* for further discussion on Holy Relationships)

There is no hurry for us to begin practicing miracles. We have a long time – eternity, in fact—to choose to let go of and undo our guilt and shame. What is more, Wapnick (1990) says, "The Course does not require... that we understand the metaphysics of time [see e.g. Workbook Lesson 169]; it merely asks that we understand the importance of choosing a miracle."

Miracle principle 13 says, "Miracles are both beginnings and endings, and so they alter the temporal order. .... They undo the past in the present, and thus release the future." (4T, 13:1-3) Our job is thus only to *ask for* the miracle, at which point the Holy Spirit does the rest: "Extension of [miracles and] forgiveness is the Holy Spirit's function." As we learn the Course's message at a progressively deeper level, we discover that *time*, like this incarnation in general, is a *classroom* where we learn to choose God.

As we heal, we ask the Holy Spirit for help, which the Course says is all that we have to do to initiate a miracle. It is then the Holy Spirit's job to do the rest, as we remain open (through *willingness* and *humility*) to God's Love, which is already and always within us, as us. As shown in Figure1 in the first chapter, through practicing miracles and forgiveness, we let God/Holy Spirit/Christ assist us as we remove our blocks to "...the awareness of love's presence, which is [our] natural inheritance." (T, introduction:7)

The goal of the Course is for us to experience God's Love, which is there underneath the blocks to our awareness of It. God's Love, the Holy Spirit, *is* the real world, which we facilitate when we have an attitude of forgiveness, or letting go of our ego and its world. I discuss the real world further in chapter 6.

The real world, or seeing with Christ's vision, has at least 12 aspects or characteristics, as shown in Figure 1 of the first Chapter. In its crazy dream, the ego has attempted to surmount each of these 12 aspects of God's real world with illusory replacements, and one of these is time. The ego tries to use time to deny and replace eternity. But the Holy Spirit gently undoes the ego's world of separation, time and belief in sin by making our need for linear time unnecessary, as we settle into the peace of the holy instant – each time that we choose God.

THE END OF TIME

A conventional Christian view is that in time, the world will end in judgment, fire, or what it calls "Armageddon." But the Course says that instead it will end in forgiveness, and will include all of God's children. Our final lesson is thus letting go of our belief in and attachment to the ego and its crazy world. We thereby accept "the peace of God" and the Atonement for ourself, which is also the Second Coming, which I

23

discussed in Chapter 12 of *Choosing God*. We learn that there is nothing in linear time or in the outside world but our own projections, and we can eventually forgive/let go of both the ego and its world *and ourself* for buying into it in the first place.

The Course says that God does not judge us: "Judgment is not an attribute of God." (34T, 2:3) Rather, as the ego's world ends, the Holy Spirit gently corrects our ego-oriented judgmental belief in separation and attack. The Course also re-interprets the "Apocalypse" (which meant "secret" or "revealed writings") as our own *right-mindedness* each time that we experience God's truth when we choose God, as opposed to the ego's illusions. The "last" judgment is thus when we accept this difference at last, and now see with Christ's vision. It says that the only "judgment" that the Holy Spirit makes is when it differentiates between expressions of God's Love or calls for It.

The Course says that the purpose of time is only to give us "time" to achieve this judgment: "God's Judgment is the gift of the Correction He bestowed on all your errors, freeing you from them, and all effects they ever seemed to have. To fear God's saving grace is but to fear complete release from suffering, return to peace, security and happiness, and union with your own Identity. ... Be not afraid of love. ... This is God's final Judgment: 'You are still my holy Son [Daughter], forever innocent, forever loving, and forever loved, as limitless as your Creator, and completely changeless and forever pure. Therefore awaken and return to me. I am your Father and you are my Son/[Daughter].' " (455W, 3-5)

Yet the Course uses terms to fit into our familiarity with linear time, perhaps so that we can begin to understand its message better. It thus enters the dream world of illusion, while helping us realize the truth beyond illusion. These terms include "God's last step," "Second Coming of Christ," and God's "last judgment," each of which's meaning I summarize in Table 5 Meanings of Terms Describing the End of Time .

Term	Actual Meaning according to ACIM
God's Last Step	God's original and only **creation** of Christ/Sonship/[Daughtership] (i.e., all of us). Re-awakening in our mind of the separated Son to his Oneness as Christ.
Second Coming of Christ	**Our** individual and collective **re-awakening** to Christ's vision, which is the "return of sense," or realizing God's real world.
Last Judgment	Our acceptance of our own right-mindedness and Christhood, as God's holy Son/[Daughter], forever innocent, sinless, loving, loved, eternal, peaceful, limitless, changeless and pure. (455W, 5; 38M, 1:1-12)
Revelation	Our experience when we choose and remember God
Apocalypse	Sorting out the false (ego) from the true (God) (34T, 4:2). Same as Last Judgment.
"Armageddon"	Not mentioned directly in the Course, which indirectly refers to the gentle way the world will end as including all of the above, brought about individually through forgiveness, and includes all of God's Children (Wapnick 1990)

Table 5.
Meanings of Terms Describing the End of Time *

* In the table we can see that while each of these terms may appear slightly different on the surface, they actually mean the same thing. This is because they all describe the end of our ego dream and our experiential re-awakening to our own personal and collective Christhood.

25

There are also the three terms from conventional Christianity that are related to the end of "time": Apocalypse and Armageddon, which I describe at the bottom of Table 4 above, and revelation. To me, all six of these terms can be misused by the ego to promote more separation, fear, guilt and shame, or alternatively, each time that we choose God, they can be used by the Holy Spirit to gently move us into the peace of Eternal Now, which the Course calls the holy instant (capitalized or not).

The Course summarized the notion of the end of time by saying that there is no last step for God to take, since God created everything perfect. "God does not take steps, because His accomplishments are not gradual. He does not teach, because His creations are changeless. He does nothing last because He created first and for always." (113T, 7:1-3) Thus, no matter what we may call it, God's final step, which the Course refers to metaphorically, is really His first, only, and eternal creation, which we experientially enter each time that we choose God.

SUMMARY

The Course says a lot about time. In review -- and, as well, to mention a few of its aspects that I have not covered above -- I list some of time's characteristics in Table 6 below.

Our choice	Everything in it changes
We chose and made it to support our belief in separation, sin, guilt and death.	A teaching, learning and healing device to heal he separation and use time constructively
The ego's concept; began at the separation	Our friend, if we choose God
Pain preserves and binds time	Miracles save us time
A meaningless illusion	Will be as we interpret it
Chosen by the choice-maker in our mind.	Neutral, as the body and physical universe
The mind -- Our observer/decision-/choice maker is outside of time and space	Can release or imprison us
The insane belief that the past is still here and now	We don't need to understand its metaphysics to benefit from the Course
Opposite of eternity	A means to regain eternity
Has no effect on eternity	*Now* is its only eternal aspect.

Table 6.

Some Characteristics of Time from ACIM

What is healing but the removal of all that stands in the way of knowledge?

A Course in Miracles p 188

4 PRAYER

Prayer helps us co-create miracles. It helps us know ourself, others and God, and heal. While the Course mentions it throughout, it does so the most in two sections of Chapters 3 and 9 in the Text (45T, 6:6-10; 163–166T) and in the beginning section of "The Song of Prayer," which is a booklet that Helen received and scribed after the Course.

Prayer is the medium of miracles (45T, 6:2). When we initiate a miracle, we may first feel a need for help from God. Then we may remember that we have a choice, and then we pray. I list some of the Course's description of the characteristics of prayer in Table 7.

While there are different kinds of prayer, the Course says that the only meaningful prayer is when we ask to recognize what we already have. It calls this "praying for forgiveness," because those who have been forgiven have everything (45T, 6:3, 5).

Table7.

Characteristics of Prayer from ACIM & "The Song of Prayer"

God's greatest gift	Letting go, quiet listening and loving
A ladder reaching to Heaven	Giving up self to be one with Love
Involves levels of learning	Shared love
Medium of miracles	Way to humility
Directed by Holy Spirit under the laws of God	Part of life and forgiveness

Way to reach and remember God and our holiness	Extends creation
Can bring God's peace	Means to oneness
Part of us and God	Sister to forgiveness
Always answered	Always for ourself (as is forgiveness)

THE LADDER OF PRAYER

In the booklet "The Song of Prayer," prayer is described as a ladder that has levels that are components of the process of healing. At the lowest level we may pray for any externals that we may desire, such as status, things, and the love of others, as shown in Table 8. But doing so will only imprison us, since these externals are a substitute for God, and thereby distort the purpose of prayer (65S, 3). Also, praying for specifics always asks to have the past repeated in some way. Rather, "The aim of prayer is to release the present from its chains of past illusions; to let it be a freely-chosen remedy from every choice that stood for a mistake. What prayer can offer now so far exceeds all that you asked before that it is pitiful to be content with less." (7S, 2)

The next rung on the ladder involves praying *for* others, including our enemies. This kind of prayer can be useful. In fact, it has been shown by scientific studies to be effective for people with illness when unknown others pray for them (e.g., Byrd 1988, Benor 1990, Dossey 1993.)

Next is praying *with* others. Similar to group meditation's ability to make an individual's meditation deeper, praying with others is a higher and more effective kind of prayer. Yet, paradoxically, the Course says that prayer is always for ourself.

The next level is to pray for help in healing the *cause* of *fear*. Rather than praying for release from fear, the Course suggests that it is more constructive to pray for help in healing and releasing fear's cause.

A still higher form of prayer is praying for God's Will. In the Twelve Steps of AA and other self-help fellowships, the Eleventh Step says, "Sought through prayer and meditation to improve our conscious contact with God, as we understood Him, praying only for knowledge of His will for us and the power to carry that out."

The final and top rung in the ladder of prayer is praying to see the Christ in others and our self. This is when we can begin to achieve a Christ consciousness, i.e., to see with the vision or eyes of Christ. As described in Chapter 15 of my previous book *Choosing God*, on "Perception and Knowledge", Christ's vision is true perception coming from our right mind, which is guided by the Holy Spirit. Realizing Christ's vision is our only task on our path to Knowledge. Once we have seen through the eyes of Christ, we "need do nothing," since God does the rest in His last step to take us home to Heaven, which is pure being in God's Love. The latter is both the goal and the way to reach the goal, as shown at the top of Table 2.

Table 8a.
The Ladder of Prayer—the process of healing
reads best from bottom

Reality ⟷ Pure Being in God's Love

Content	Goal & Way Home/Heaven/Formless Silence		
Actions to Achieve	*Praying for - (Levels)*	*Results*	*Jesus as*
5) Defenselessness	*Seeing Christ in others and self		* Brother -- Goal: Christ's vision
4) Trust	↑ * God's Will for us *Help in healing our cause of fear	Peace	* Model
3) Prayer *with* others	↑ * With others	↑ brings	
2) Faith	↑ * Others, including our enemies		* Teacher
1) A little willingness	↑ * Any external: status, things, others' love ...will imprison us	↑ Humility* "Special" -" the only Son of God"	

Table 8b.
The unreality of the ego's world.
Contrasting with Table 8a.

World of Form	ego's world *Distractions/Illusion*	
ego's arrogance	**sin *guilt *fear	*some religious ritual
... Plan to usurp & replace God & His Kingdom		
Duality *Body/World	*Specialness *Viciousness	*Defensiveness — including esp. dissociation & projection

CONTENT VERSUS FORM IN PRAYER

The Course describes God and God's world as reality and "content," as opposed to the ego and its world as being unreal and "form" (see left side of Table 8). To navigate God's world related to prayer we can practice the four actions of : 1) having a little willingness, 2) faith, 3) trust, and 4) defenselessness. As lesson 153 of the workbook addresses, practicing these characteristics of the Teachers of God will bring about humility and eventually inner peace, as shown in Table 8a. Table 8b shows a contrast to the healing tenets of the Ladder of Prayer in table 8a.

These four actions and two results, humility and inner peace, are parallel and are a part of the kinds of prayer on the ladder. Still another action —the way we see Jesus – also parallels these. We can see Jesus first as special, i.e. as the *only* son of God, which is usually the way most conventional Christian denominations see him. The author of the Course, Jesus/Christ/Christ consciousness, says that a more accurate way of seeing him is as our *brother*. In this sense we are more his peer and thus potentially equal to him, as we evolve to realizing our ability to see with his vision.

Finally, he goes a step further. He says that as we see that he is our brother and that we are all one as the Christ, we will no longer see him as a separate being, and thus even he will become an illusion.

The above has described some important aspects of God and God's world, which the Course also calls *reality* or *content*. By contrast, it also describes the unreality or *form* of the ego and its world, as shown at the bottom left of Table 8. These aspects of the ego are both distractions and illusions, and include the ego's arrogance of attachment to sin, guilt/shame and fear, plus some religious ritual (Wapnick 1998). The ego's arrogance can also be summarized as "the ego's plan to usurp and replace God and his Kingdom."

The ego sees *duality*, not the Oneness of Christ's vision. Duality includes focusing on the body and world, specialness, defensiveness (including especially dissociation and projection), and the ego's worst behavior, viciousness.

Prayer and the other components of God's world are the way out of these distractions and the insanity of the ego. Each time that we are in conflict or pain, all we need do is to choose God through prayer, meditation, or communion with God.

Each time that we choose God, we experience a miracle. Having experienced an endless string of miracles, we will eventually end experiencing ourself as pure being in God's love, at last at home in Heaven which is here and now, in the holy instant.

The Course says that communion, not prayer, is the natural state of those who know. It says, "God and his miracle are inseparable. How beautiful indeed are the thoughts of God who live in His light! Your worth is beyond perception because it is beyond doubt. Do not perceive yourself in different lights. Know yourself in the One Light where the miracle that is you is perfectly clear." (46T, 10:5-9)

Let forgiveness be the substitute for fear.
This is the only rule for happy dreams.

A Course in Miracles p 590

5 THE BODY

In helping us answer the perennial questions "Who am I?, What am I doing here?, and Where am I going?", spiritual masters and sages have suggested that we are not our body. Yet they say that we can use our body to evolve.

The Course has a similar message in the way that it describes the body. It says that our body is a part of our existence in the physical world. While it is ultimately an illusion, we can use it as another teaching device as we journey Home.

When we look on our body and the bodies of others, we can do so with our wrong mind or our right mind. To look through our wrong mind is when we look through our ego, which the Course says is the body's symbol, idol, friend and home. Looking through our ego –and thus our wrong mind, we see only differences, separation, and are prone to attack. Indeed, the body is the central figure in our dream of this world. It is the way the ego tries to make special (unholy) relationships, in part by seeing only form through the body's eyes or characteristics, as shown in part in Table 9.

Alone, the body has no function. But when our right mind uses it for the goals of the Holy Spirit, it can become a communication device. In this way our body does only what our mind directs it to do: it receives and sends the messages that we give it via our mind.

Like the world, the body is a paradox. It can be helpful when we use it constructively:

"You can use your body best to help you enlarge your perception so you can achieve real vision, of which the physical eye is incapable. Learning to do this is the body's only true usefulness." (12T/15T, 2:4-5)

37

Accomplishing real vision, i.e., Christ's vision, will come easily when we choose God over our ego, since our body easily aligns with our right mind. Miracles also transcend our body, and allow us to be sane and at peace when we extend our spirit to our brother.

When we use our body destructively, which is through our ego/wrong mind, we end up feeling painful feelings, such as fear, anger and guilt/shame and creating special relationships. Our body thus acts wrongly when our wrong mind directs it.

The Course says that God did not make our body because it is destructible and thus not of God's world. While our body is a separation device and a symbol of what we think we are, ultimately it does not exist. But while we have it, the Holy Spirit translates it into a learning device by reinterpreting the ego's use of it for separation into the unity of minds. Miracles show us that our mind can heal our body when we choose God over our ego. (105T, 2:1-7)

Part of our existence in the physical world	Receives and sends the messages we give it; it does only what our mind directs
A framework for developing abilities	Acts wrongly when responds to wrong mind
Is outside of us, yet seems to surround, shut off & keep us apart	Easily aligns with right mind
Does not separate us	Holy Spirit directs its use
An attempt to limit communication	Cannot make itself sick or heal itself
A communication device; a means, not an end	A tiny fence around a little part of a glorious & complete idea
Cannot feel, know or forgive	Not joined with others (minds are)
Differences are only of it	A limit on love; awareness of it makes love seem limited
Symbol, idol, friend & home of ego & of what we think we are	Guilt's messenger
Ego uses it to separate and attack for power	A learning aid (like miracles) to facilitate a state wherein it becomes unnecessary
Harmful to us if we use it for attack	We feel lonely & deprived when we perceive it as our reality
Central figure in our dream of the world	Not part of us
Way ego tries to make the unholy [special] relationship	Can't access our spirit or solve anything
Its eyes see only form	No function alone
It seems whatever we [perceive] it to be	A dream, not real
Its condition [depends] on our interpretation [perception] of it	A way to be sane when we extend love to our brother
Mind's perception and use makes it healthy or sick	A vehicle that helps us choose the freedom of the Holy Spirit

Table 9.

Characteristics of the Body from ACIM

Our mind becomes free when we no longer see ourself as being in a body. The ego holds the body dear, and lives and hides in it. Lesson 199 on page 382 in the Workbook says that when we choose God over our ego our body disappears, because we have no need of it except for what the Holy Spirit sees. Now the body becomes a vehicle that helps forgiveness be extended to the all-inclusive goal that it must reach, according to God's plan. When we declare our innocence and choose the freedom of the Holy Spirit, we can then carry it as our gift to our brothers and sisters. By doing so, we let love replace our fear, knowing that God extends His Love and happiness when we say:

I am not a body. I am free. I hear the Voice that God has given me, and it is only this my mind obeys. (383W, 8:6-9)

The Course also says, "God did not make the body, because it is destructible, and therefore not of the Kingdom." (105T, 2:1)

In the next chapter I describe how the Course sees the world, which is similar to how it describes the body. In Table 10 I show how it sees both the body and the world from the views of right and wrong mind.

Views --->	*Right Mind*	*Wrong Mind*
Body **and** **World**	Holy Spirit's teaching devices through which we learn forgiveness	ego attached Reinforces separation

Table 10.
The Body and World as seen by Right and wrong Mind

40

In Table 11 below I further summarize how it sees the body and the world from the views of Levels One and Two, plus a summary of how it describes time and perception.

	Level One	*Level Two*
Body	Embodiment of the ego; mind's thought of separation projected into form; includes our personality	Inherently neutral, neither "good" nor "evil"; its purpose is given it by our mind
World	As a body, the mind's thought of separation given form; *our* perception; not created by God, Who transcends form, space and time	Here, through our conflicts, we can learn about letting go of ego and choosing God
Time	Contained in a tiny instant – already corrected by the Holy Spirit	Allows choice of focusing on past and future or living in the holy instant, the time interval of miracles
Perception	Post-separation world of form & differences, arising from our belief in separation	From projecting our inner pain, which results in our interpretation of "reality"; may be wrong-or right-minded

Table 11.

Terms Described as Levels One and Two in ACIM
(as interpreted by Wapnick 1989)

6 THE WORLD

In *Choosing God,* I said that forgiveness has been the most difficult idea in the Course for me to understand.[3] I believe that the Course's references to "the world" are second to forgiveness in a level of difficulty for me to grasp. For example, does the Course mean *planet Earth* when it refers to the world? After reflecting on this question for a while and re-reading the Course some more, my answer to this question is both "yes" and "no." Let me explain.

The Course makes reference to the "earth" about 111 times. (Concordance 1997, p 227) References to the earth are usually made in contrast to heaven, and reflect that the earth is a classroom in which we can grow. I have read some sections of the Course where I could consider that when it mentions "the world" that it may be referring to our planet.

For example:

"Salvation is no more than a reminder that this world is not your home." (530T, 6:1) and "This world you live in is not home to you…. We speak today for everyone who walks this world, for he is not at home." (339W, 1:1, 3:1)

---

[3] In Chapter 17 of *Choosing God* I said, For me, forgiveness has been the most difficult idea to understand in the Course. This is because it is discussed in such a circular manner throughout its three volumes that it is hard to find a section that defines it clearly and comprehensively. Like many of its readers, I've had to dig it out by reading, re-reading and then focusing on any sections where it is mentioned more than just in passing.

On one level, these words could be referring to planet Earth. Terms like "home," "live in," and "walks" may suggest our physical planet as possibly being "this world." But most of the time when I read it, paying close attention to the *context* of the passage, I am able to differentiate *this* meaning from a more common and more *metaphorical* meaning, in which it refers to the world not as planet Earth, but as the ego's world.

The Course says that the body is inherently neutral, being neither "good" nor "evil." Rather, its purpose is given it by the mind. To our wrong mind it is a source of fear, guilt/shame and attack. To our right mind it is a learning device for peace and forgiveness. My sense is that the world as planet Earth is similar. It is inherently neutral, and these same above qualities of the body fit a description of it as well. The Course refers to the world as constituting an entity of space, time and form, that which we see with our physical eyes. Our physical eyes may see the world as being neutral (less commonly) or as a place and cause of pain, suffering and death (most commonly), which is usually seen (i.e.,filtered) through the ego. The Course says:

"The world you see is the delusional system of those made mad by guilt. Look carefully at this world, and you will realize that this is so. For this world is the symbol of punishment, and all the laws that seem to govern it are the laws of death. Children are born into it through pain and in pain. Their growth is attended by suffering, and they learn of sorrow and separation and death. ... If this were the real world, God *would* be cruel. (236T, 2:2-6; 3:1)

But the Course contrasts this world, which is also called the ego's world, with God's real world. The ego's world comes about through our dream of separation, which has its basis in and rests on sin and scarcity. Through our false perception (wrong mind), it distracts and deceives us, leaving us in pain. Although it is not real, the ego's world's purpose is to prove that guilt and shame are real, and we believe in it and fear it, as shown in table 10.

Characteristic	ego's world	God's Real World
Reality	Not real	Real
Origin	Dream of separation	Gift of the Holy Spirit
Rests on	Sin and scarcity	Unity and health
Description	Distracts, deceives & is merciless	Timeless and changeless
Perception	False	True; loving thoughts
Attain by	Ego, wrong mind	Right mind; forgiving ego's world
Purpose	Prove guilt/shame real	Forgiveness
Feeling	Pain	Peace
Result	Disappoints us; we believe and fear it	We may not believe it, yet it is ours for the asking. Leads us to remember God

Table 12.
Two Worlds, Contrasted

If we look upon planet Earth and its vast nature through our physical eyes alone, this (the ego's world in the center column of Table 12) is what we see. But if we look at this same planet through the eyes of Christ (Christ's vision), we can see God's real world (right column), which is the

45

gift of the Holy Spirit. The real world has its basis in unity and health, and like God and Heaven, is formless, timeless and changeless. Through quiet eyes, we can "see" (i.e., experience) the real world when we are in our right mind, using what the Course calls true perception. We can attain our experience of right mind and peace each time that we co-create a miracle by asking God/Holy Spirit/Christ for help. By so doing, we are asking the Holy Spirit to help us let go of (i.e., forgive) the ego's world. While we may not believe in it, the real world is ours for the asking, since experiencing it leads us to remember God.

EGO ATTEMPTS TO DENY ITS PROJECTION

In volume one of *The Message of a Course in Miracles*, Ken Wapnick describes how we first experience the world within our mind, and then project that experience outside as *special relationships* with and through 1) our own body, 2) others and even with 3) planet Earth. Our ego's thought of separation projects itself (i.e., the idea of separation) onto the body, the world and the physical universe for two purposes: 1) to hide the separation that we made in our own mind, and 2) to protect its ego self from the mind's inevitable decision for choosing the Holy Spirit over it (Wapnick 1997).

In a strange but not unexpected maneuver (knowing the ego), the ego then tries to deny its above-described projection and reverse that truth. It claims that the physical world, i.e., the body, world and physical universe, caused the thought/idea/existence of separation. Its purpose in this reversal is to reinforce our belief in the body/world/physical universe. This idea of separation also promotes our belief in sin, guilt/shame and fear, which now continues to bolster our belief in the physical, thereby strengthening the ego's imagined fortress against God, as shown in Table 13. (Wapnick 1997)

True/False?	Cause	Projection	Effect	ego's Purpose
True	ego/ thought of separation	Projected onto →	The body/world/ physical universe	Hide the separation & protect itself from mind's inevitable decision for God
ego then attempts to reverse the truth:				
False	Body/ world/ physical universe	← Projected onto	Thought of separation	To reinforce our belief in the body/world/ physical universe (ego's fortress against God)

Table 13.

Construction of the ego's world

DID GOD MAKE PLANET EARTH?

It has been difficult and confusing for me (as my ego? my past assumptions?) to accept that God did not make the physical world as planet Earth and nature, but I am slowly coming to more seriously consider that possibility.

Contrary to all of our Judeo-Christian religious teachings, the Course says that God did *not* make anything physical that our ordinary eyes can see. Where does that leave us with the way we view the world as nature? My answer is that it leaves our relationships with people, places and things open as "grist for the mill" of our psycho-spiritual development. We can look on any of these with our physical eyes/ego/wrong mind and see and experience special relationships, bodies and the pain of the ego's world. Or we can see them with Christ's vision/spirit (our real self)/right mind and see holy relationships and the real world of God – and thereby experience peace. The way that we do the latter is to co-create miracles, one at a time.

From this perspective we can now begin to see the body and the world differently. And as we do that we can slowly reconsider our prior assumptions and experiences with them from levels one and two as presented in the Course, and summarized in Table 14.

From a level *one* perspective, both the body and the world are the effects of the thought of separation projected by the mind into form. Neither was created by God, who transcends form, space and time. *No matter how perplexing or confusing* these ideas may be to us, the Course says that *we don't need to figure them out*, or even *try* to do so. That is not our job. In fact, *nothing* in level one is *our responsibility,* task, or burden. That is all God's job. So from my understanding of the Course, we can simply *let go and observe* the Divine Mystery unfold from a level one perspective – even while we are exposed to a level two influence or temptation.

Beginning of Level One:
Thought of separation projected by the mind into form.

Level	*Body*	*World*
One	ego's embodiment; seeming witness to "reality" of the separation	Not created by God, Who transcends time and space
Two	*wrong* mind —symbol of guilt/shame & attack	Separated world reinforces ego's belief in sin & guilt, perpetuating the world's seeming existence
	Right mind —Instrument of learning forgiveness and salvation, whereby we learn to transcend them both.	

Table 14.

The Body and the World According to Levels One and Two from
ACIM

(also compiled from Wapnick 1989)

We can now use our experience of people, places and things in level two to further our psycho-spiritual growth. We can use this – as we co-create miracles – as instruments of learning forgiveness, salvation and peace, and thereby gradually transcend our attachments to them.

As we heal, we slowly learn to "see" (i.e., experience) the world differently. We can now see the world as a teaching and learning device to realize 1) forgiveness, 2) that planet Earth is not our home, 3) that the ego's world is not our home, and 4) thus heal, which is all the world is for.

Robert Perry said, "Nature is not our home. It is not a fitting residence for a Son of God. It is a war in progress. But there is room to love and appreciate it. It is our task to love and take care of our other brothers, the trillions of broken pieces of God's Son that lie behind the myriad forms of nature. And it is our task to see nature's beautiful forms as dream symbols of the transcendent beauty that our physical eyes will never see." (Perry 1998)

We now know that we have the ability to begin to see both the body and the world differently. And as we do that, we can consider how our own healing takes place.

7 HEALING

The Course says that healing is all that the world is for. But to understand healing, we need first to understand sickness.

SICKNESS IS WRONG-MINDEDNESS

The Course says that sickness has little or nothing to do with the body. (398T, 3:1-3; 18M, 3:2) Rather, sickness is a decision that the mind makes when it chooses the ego instead of God. Sickness is thus the ego's interpretation that we are a body, and that our body is for attack. Sickness is anger taken out on the body. If we buy into the ego's interpretation, we can end up believing that we can be hurt.

But by his resurrection some 2,000 years ago, and in our own resurrections today, one of Christ's central teachings is that we are not a body and that we cannot be hurt (discussed on page 80 ff of *Choosing God*.) In this sense, we can see sickness as being an illusion. Indeed, perhaps sickness's only usefulness is to show us that our mind is currently split, and that we are choosing our ego over God. The Course says that sickness is also the physical expression of our fear of awakening and healing, which becomes a symbol of our deciding against God.

Sickness comes from separation, while healing comes from joining. Sickness is a call for love and health. Coming from our wrong mind, it is a faulty approach to solving problems and conflicts. In fact, we made sickness as a kind of god, which the Course calls "the god of sickness," with which we are at war and strangely worship at the same time.

From his study and understanding of the Course since Helen and Bill brought it to us, Ken Wapnick defines sickness as "a conflict in the mind (guilt) displaced onto the body." It is "the ego's attempt to defend itself against truth (spirit) by focusing attention on the body." Furthermore, in our special relationships we can blame others for our illness and pain,

51

since "a sick body is the effect of the... split mind that caused it, representing the ego's desire to make others guilty by sacrificing oneself, projecting responsibility for the attack onto them." (Wapnick 1989)

THE PROCESS OF HEALING

Healing is all the world is for, and we need healing to understand ourself. One of its most revealing quotes in this regard is, "Healing is accomplished the instant the sufferer no longer sees any value in pain." (17M,1:1)

The Course says that healing is not mysterious. But when I read the statement that "the body needs no healing" (398T, 3:2), I was confused. I also read that the body cannot heal, because it cannot make itself sick. Later, when I read that healing is the mind working through the body, I began to understand it and more. I eventually saw how sickness and healing can be more easily understood by looking at them again from a perspective of *levels*. For example, at level one, sickness is an illusion made by wrong-mindedness, and healing is therefore unnecessary, as shown in table 13. Even so, in level two, healing can occur when we ask God/Holy Spirit to help us release from fear, guilt and shame (i.e., all of our suffering.) By thus being right-minded, we can realize that mind is the only creative level (26T, 5:2), and choose God over our ego. Elsewhere the Course says that healing is not creating; it is *reparation*. (75T, 1:1)

Level	Sickness	Healing
One	An illusion made by wrong-mindedness	Unnecessary (e.g.,, 591T, 10:8)[4]*
Two	*Wrong* mind: the totality of our painful experience when we choose our ego (see text also)	If person is temporarily inaccessible to the Atonement, we may give an outside factor healing belief (see text also)
	Right mind: does not make sickness	Realizing mind is the only creative level, chooses God

Table 15.
Sickness and Healing according to Levels in ACIM

---

[4] * In Level 2, healing can occur by release from fear and guilt/shame.

The Course does not say that factors outside our mind, such as conventional and complimentary medicine or psychotherapy, are not useful. Indeed, it clearly says that at times they may help:

"Sometimes the illness has a sufficiently strong hold over the mind to render a person temporarily inaccessible to the Atonement. In this case it may be wise to utilize a compromise approach to mind and body, in which something from the outside is given healing belief. This is because the last thing that can help the non-right-minded, or the sick, is an increase in fear."(24T, 4:5-7) This is why, in part, I do not recommend jumping too deeply into the Course or any other spiritual path too deeply and too soon when the person has not first stabilized their problem or illness in a Stage One recovery program (Whitfield 1993, 95). I discuss this approach in more detail in *Choosing God*, Chapter 8.

HEALING THROUGH MIRACLES

Healing comes about through miracles. The miracle is the *means* of healing, Atonement is the *principle*, and healing is the *result*.(23T, 1:2) So we can say that if we have a conflict, pain, or sickness, we can co-create miracles, and through the Holy Spirit's job and action of bringing about Atonement, when we ask It for help, we will experience healing.

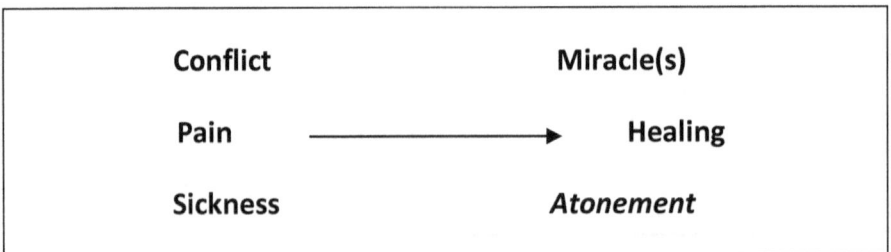

Conflict	Miracle(s)
Pain ⟶	Healing
Sickness	*Atonement*

Healing is God's gift to us, which we cannot lose. It happens when we replace fear with love. That love is the love of Christ for God and Self, all four of which (love, Christ [Self] and God) are inside of each of us. As a release from the past (guilt) and the future (fear), healing happens when we stay in the *holy instant*, which is where we are already and always, and that release of pain is the result of a miracle. Healing thus reflects the joint will of Christ and us, since it is the way in which the separation is overcome, which is through joining or unity. (145T, 5: 1-5)

Free will is key here. The living Christ, who authored the Course, says that his will is as free and powerful as ours, and that his decision cannot therefore overcome ours, although he can offer us strength to make our will invincible.(145T, 5:9-14) So we have a choice at any and all times to go with God, which brings about a miracle, which then results in healing. What makes choosing God so easy and effective when we can remember to do it, is that God's Will is the same as Christ's *and ours.* God's will for us is that we be co-creative with Him and that we have complete peace and joy.(143T, 1:1) Under these conditions -- when we are so co-creative with God resulting in complete peace and joy -- it is hard for me to imagine developing an illness.

In this world, healing is the Holy Spirit's form of communication, since the Holy Spirit originated as God's idea of healing. The Course says that when we communicate, through our mind (i.e., think loving thoughts), and join with the minds of others, we heal. Healing is the result of using the body solely for communication.(153T, 10:1) "To communicate is to join and to attack is to separate."(153T, 12:1) Our mind cannot be made physical, but it can be made manifest *through* the physical if it uses the body to go beyond itself.(153T, 10:4)

Thus the Course says that healing rests on "charity," which is a way of *perceiving* the *perfection* of our brother/sister. It is therefore a way of forgetting the fear, i.e., any sense of danger or suffering, that the ego induced in us, by not recognizing it in another. While it is not our task to heal others, our own healing will extend to others and be brought to our other problems, as well as problems we thought were not our own. (578T, 9:1-2)

The Course says that we need healing because we do not understand ourself. One of the most useful lines in the Course, for me, addresses the role of *true perception* in self-understanding and the healing process:

"Because you see them [i.e., our brothers and sisters] as they are, you offer them your acceptance of their truth so they can accept it for themselves. This is the healing that the miracle induces." "39T, 6:6-7/35)

Over my long career as a physician and psychotherapist, I have seen this happen over and over. Whether it is in individual therapy, group therapy, or Twelve Step or other self-help group process, this is a key ingredient in healing. **When others accept us and our experience as we are, and how it is for us *when we are real* in telling our story — we can finally accept it for ourself, grieve our pain, and let go of it.**

A LESSON IN UNDERSTANDING

Healing thus becomes a lesson in understanding self, others and God. By healing we learn of our wholeness, from which we learn to remember God. The more we practice it, the better we become in learning even more about healing and teaching it. The beginning of our return to knowledge, healing proves that the separation is without lasting effect. Before the separation, there was no need for healing.

Healing recognizes that wills are joined, and it sees no specialness. It undoes our belief in differences and is the only way to perceive the Sonship as one. It involves a *thought* by which two minds perceive their oneness and become glad. No matter who initiates the healing process, both/all parties involved receive equal benefit.

56

Healing comes from God's power and only strengthens us, yet we have to be vulnerable to ask for it. We ask to heal in the present so that we can release the past and the future. When we accept that sickness is a decision of our mind (when it chooses ego), we can begin to heal. (18M, 2:1) Each time that we choose God, we will begin to see the world and others differently.

Ideas leave not their source.

Change your mind about yourself and healing will follow.

A Course in Miracles 311 T

8 TEACHERS OF GOD

The Course says that we are each a teacher of God, as well as a student, as we learn to change the only thing we need to change —our mind. To *be* a teacher of God, similar to choosing God in the unfolding of a miracle, we simply *choose* to be one.

TEACHING AND LEARNING

Since teacher and learner are the same, we slowly discover that to teach is also to learn. We learn that we always have two choices—our ego or God. Which do we want? Do we want to learn and have peace and joy, or conflict and pain? The Course gives us a way to teach based on what we *want* to learn. One of the things that we learn is that we cannot give to someone else, but only to ourself —each time that we choose God— and we also learn that lesson by teaching it. (1M, 2:5-6)

HAVING HUMILITY

The Course says that a key to learning is being *humble*, having humility, which I described in *Choosing God* as being open to learning about self, others and God, and in more detail with my co-authors in *The Power of Humility*. Eastern spiritual approaches such as Buddhism have addressed humility in their powerful concept and practice often referred to as "don't know." Both a Twelve Step approach and the Course see our attachment to our ego as our major stumbling block to true knowledge and peace. The ego, which the Course also calls wrong mind, thinks it knows it all, which is a key problem if we attach ourselves to it. Pain is our usual result.

The Course offers a way out of this unnecessary pain. It says, "Your part is very simple. You need only recognize that everything you learned you do not want. Ask to be taught, and do not use your experiences to confirm what you have learned. When your peace is threatened or disturbed in any way, say to yourself:

"I do not know what anything, including this, means. And so I do not know how to respond to it. And I will not use my own past learning as the light to guide me now.

"By this refusal to attempt to teach yourself what you do not know, the Guide Whom God has given you will speak to you. He will take His rightful place in your awareness the instant you abandon it, and offer it to Him." (297T, 6:3-11).

What it is suggesting here is that we can each peresonally experience a miracle, or the whole loving and usually ultimately peaceful experience of choosing God/Holy Spirit/Christ over the ego.

In the Workbook for Students, Lesson 182 addresses humility as becoming as a little Child to God as we are healthily dependent upon and humble in our relationship with God. This lesson powerfully expands upon what Jesus said in the New Testament: "I tell you, unless you change and become like little children, you will never enter the kingdom of heaven." (Matt 18:3; also in Matt 19:14, Luke 18:16-17 and the Thomas Gospel)

LETTING GO OF BELIEFS AND JUDGMENTS

A second key to teaching and learning is in our *believing.* Our beliefs come from our experience, which is based on our perceptions and judgments. Our perception—or false perception—and judgment come from our ego, wherein we learn and experience a world of conflict and pain. But we always have a choice. We can "choose once again" when we ask to see through the eyes of Christ, which is true perception, and give our judgment over to the Holy Spirit. As shown in Table 16, this remembering and choosing is the way that we learn and then teach, as teachers of God.

Beliefs and practices of:

Term	Perception	Judgment
ego's	False perception	Judging self and others [5]
God's	True perception (Christ's vision)	Letting Holy Spirit judge, i.e., translate fear into love, which is God's gift of the Correction He bestowed on all our mistakes (455W, 3-5)

Table 16.
The Basis of Learning and Teaching

---

[5] I describe more on true and false perception in Chapter 15 of *Choosing God*: A Bird's-eye-view of *ACIM*.

THE TEACHERS

Teachers of God come from all of the religions of the world and from no religion. They answer God's Call to learn and teach (both of which mean to *remember*) the central theme of the Holy Spirit's universal curriculum: that we are innocent and without guilt or shame —and that we are all One, and that we never left God. We can teach this message by numerous ways, including in our thoughts, actions, words—or no words— in any language or no language, in any place or way, and at any time. And as we so learn and teach, we save ourselves time in our process of spiritual growth, as discussed in Chapter 2 above. (3M, 3-4)

The ultimate goal of each teaching-learning situation is to make the teacher-student relationship holy, in which each can see themselves and the other as sinless. Whether we meet casually, more closely, or even intimately, all of our relationships are a potential teaching-learning situation, during which we will learn the most that we can from the other at that time. Some experiences will be brief, others longer, and some lifelong. (7-8M, 1-5) The Course says, "When you meet anyone, remember it is a holy encounter. As you see him you will see yourself. As you treat him you will treat yourself. As you think of him you will think of yourself. Never forget this, for in him you will find yourself or lose yourself." (142T, 4:1-5)

TEN CHARACTERISTICS OF GOD'S TEACHERS

We each have an ego and are different from each other in many ways, although these differences are only temporary. In our teaching-learning experience, God gives us each 10 spiritually powerful characteristics. In the Teachers Manual (which the Course formally calls the Manual for Teachers), the Course devotes seven pages to describing these characteristics of God's teachers. I have summarized my understanding of these in Table 15. They include being able to trust, be honest, tolerant, gentle, defenseless, generous, patient, faithful, and to feel joy.

62

Table 17.

Characteristics of the Teachers of God from ACIM

1) Trust	Four stages, including: * Undoing – Experiencing losses of things and relationships. * Sorting out – all experiences are real only as they are helpful in sorting out what is valuable to us. * Period of relinquishment – of the valueless. Turning the curse into the gift. * Settling down – We give up what we don't want, and keep what we do want.
2) Honesty	* Flows from trust. * Nothing we say that contradicts what we think or do (i.e., we have congruence, integrity) * No inner or outer conflict. Brings peace. * Conflict comes from self deception.
3) Tolerance	To judge is to be dishonest & implies a lack of trust. Judgment destroys honesty & trust. Being tolerant is a way out.
4) Gentleness	Harm is the outcome of judgment, the end of peace, & denial of learning, although we cannot be harmed.

5) Joy	The inevitable result of being gentle and defenseless. — See several examples below
6) Defenselessness	* Results in safety, peace, joy & God. * Defenses are but foolish guardians of insane illusions.
7) Generosity	The opposite of the world's definition, it is giving to keep not material things, but all things that are of God. Trust is the essential part of giving, that guarantees the giver will only gain.
8) Patience	Natural to those who trust
9) Faithfulness	Trust in God's word to set all problems right. Combines other teacher attributes, as gentleness, confidence, joy.
10) Open-mindedness	Comes with lack of judgment, letting Christ's image be extended to the Son. Facilitates forgiving.

In addition to these characteristics, we each have other attributes that the Course calls our *inheritance* from God, including *love, sinlessness, perfection, knowledge* and *eternal truth*. The most direct way I know to realize and experience these characteristics and attributes is always to remember to Choose God over our ego.

"Do not despair, then, because of limitations. It is your function to escape from them, but not be without them. If you would be heard by those who suffer, you must speak their language. If you would be a savior, you must understand what needs to be escaped. Salvation is not theoretical. Behold the problem, ask for the answer, and then accept it when it comes. Nor will its coming be long delayed. All the help you can accept will be provided, and not one need you have will not be met. Let us not, then, be too concerned with goals for which you are not ready. God takes you where you are and welcomes you. What more could you desire, when this is all you need?" (M, 64-5, 4-10)

As a further example of one of these characteristics of the Teachers of God, here are some statements from the Course about **joy**:

"The Holy Spirit never varies on this point, and so the one mood He engenders is joy" (109T, 1-10)

"What can be more joyous than to perceive we are deprived of nothing?" 329T, 8-3

"Joy cannot be perceived except through constant vision." 464T, 13-3

"The constancy of joy is a condition quite alien to your understanding. Yet if you could even imagine what it must be, you would desire it although you understand it not. The constancy of happiness has no exceptions; no change of any kind. It is unshakable as is the Love of God for His creation. Sure in its vision as its Creator is in what He knows, happiness looks on every thing and sees it is the same. It sees not the ephemeral, for it desires everything be like itself, and sees it so. Nothing has power to confound its constancy, because its own desire cannot be shaken. It comes as surely unto those who see the final question is necessary to the rest, as peace must come to those who choose to heal and not to judge." 465M, 2: 1-8

*　　　　*　　　　*

"Beyond the body that you interposed between you and your brother, and shining in the golden light that reaches it from the bright, endless circle that extends forever, is your holy relationship, beloved of God Himself. How still it rests, in time and yet beyond, immortal yet on earth. How great the power that lies in it. Time waits upon its will, and earth will be as it would have it be. Here is no separate will, nor the desire that anything be separate. Its will has no exceptions, and what it wills is true. Every illusion brought to its forgiveness is gently overlooked and disappears. For at its center Christ has been reborn, to light His home with vision that overlooks the world. Would you not have this holy home be yours as well? No misery is here, but only joy." 474T, 12:1-10

The ego does not want to teach everyone all it has learned, because that would defeat its purpose.

A Course in Miracles 109 T

---

9 GOD'S WILL

WHAT IS GOD'S WILL FOR US ?

An important part of our healing is remembering what we have forgotten. This remembering is a theme that runs throughout the Course. It says that we forget in order to remember Self, others and God better.(115T, 6:5) Its author, our older brother, says that we were in darkness ("The Fall," forgetting, becoming ego-attached) until any one of us realized and lived as God's Will for us, some elements of which are shown in Table 16. When we did that, it was perfectly accomplished by all. He says, "My mission was simply to unite the will of the Sonship with the Will of the Father by being aware of the Father's Will myself. This is the awareness I came to give you, and your problem in accepting it is the problem of this world." (144T, 3:4-5)

He says that healing is the way we overcome the separation and reflects our joint will. We decide to heal in our mind each time that we choose God. Even the trinity of Christ, the Holy Spirit and God cannot overcome our will, which is as free as Christ Jesus' will. All of God's children are *equal* in will, each and all being God's Will as well. "This is the only lesson I came to teach," he says. (145T, 5-6)

FREEDOM

We are each a part of God's Kingdom, and are forever free. Our freedom is reflected in the familiar term "free will." Since our freedom is in God, when we remember God we realize our freedom. Since it is love, freedom is also creation, and the Course says that it is the only gift that we can give to others.

Complete peace and joy.	Each one and all of us
To be creative with God.	Fulfilling. It is the only function we can fully experience.
Creation.	Cannot be forced on us.
Thought	God's will is our will.
Freedom.	An experience of total willingness.
Our healing.	Changeless forever.
Boundless in strength, love and peace.	The undivided will of the Sonship
Has no boundaries, because it created all things.	God wills no one suffer.

Table 18.
Some Characteristics of God's Will for Us

Our freedom lies in our Oneness, which means that we are an innate part of God, which includes God's Sonship. The Course says, "If you are part of One you mist be part of the Other, because They are One. The Holy Trinity is holy *because* It is One... [and] is everything." (146T, 8:8-11) We *are* the Will of God, and by recognizing God we recognize ourself, since we are one with God and Christ. As is our free will, our freedom is inherent within us, and cannot be learned by control, negativity or tyranny, as shown in table 19.

> **The Holy Spirit is the way God's Will is done on earth as it is in Heaven. (77T, 8:4)**
>
> **God's Will extends to us through the Holy Spirit.**

A Reason for Our Free Will

Because God made us free, He could not have imposed His Will on us without our own will and consent. The Course says that we originally and eternally accepted God's Will, since we set aside a dwelling place in us for God's Holy Spirit. While we may have temporarily forgotten that – from accepting the ego's insane reasoning to the contrary - our sound reason tells us that our will is not only part of God's Will, but that it *is* God's Will. (457T, 5: 1-11; 458T, 7: 7-12)

By learning and eventually living God's Will for us, we will learn more about the truth of our real Self. The Course says that the goal of our curriculum is "Know thyself," since there is nothing else to seek. We are each looking for our lost self, with its power and glory. (142T, 5:1-3)*

The Course continues, "God's plan is simple; never circular and never self-defeating. He has no thoughts except the Self-extending, and in this your will must be included. Thus, there must be a part of you that knows His Will and shares it."(457T, 6:1-3) It also says that the part of our mind where reason lies was dedicated, by our will in union with God's, to undoing insanity. (458T, 9:1) In my understanding of the Course, I see "reason" here as being similar to or part of Christ's vision, in that it says that reason sees no sin (but can see errors), only holy relationships. (459T, 1-11)

The only gift we can offer to others	God's Kingdom
Creation and love	Free will is God's Will
Inherent within us [in our mind]	Our freedom lies in remembering our oneness with others and God.
Our will is as free as Christ's	By offering them freedom, we are free
Cannot be learned by tyranny	Numerous other references

Table 19.
Some Characteristics of Freedom from ACIM

CONCLUSION

God has given us His Will. The Course tells us a lot about exactly what God's Will for us *is*. God wills that we each not be bound by any negativity, such as pain, suffering, "sin," or death. Indeed, God wills that we have perfect joy and happiness now, that we create with him and that we share His Love and light.

Finally, God's will is *us*, which the Course calls the Son or the Sonship, or the sum of all of God's creation, of which we are each a necessary and crucial part. Indeed, it says that without us, God is lonely, and that we are also lonely without God. It says, "God and His creations are completely dependent on Each Other. He gave them His peace so they could not be shaken and could not be deceived. ... God is lonely without His Sons, and they are lonely without Him." (22T, 5:6-8, II) Thus, God is also a *feeling* Being, who feels Love, loneliness at times, and occasionally even weeps for us (89T, 4:5). In this regard, we might ask, are feelings *human* characteristics or *Godly* ones? Perhaps they are both.

What God creates is eternal (74T, 5:6), and since God created us, we are eternal. We have nothing to fear from God, and since the ego is not real, we don't need to fear it either. So what it looks like is that most of our fear is unnecessary. We can relax. This is one of the benefits of reading the Course and practicing its principles, since it can help us experience peace. I've noticed that on the days that I read it and/or meditate, I feel better. I feel less fear, tension or conflict. For me, that's "good medicine"-- it works, *and* its free and non-toxic.

I will step back and let Him lead the way.

A Course in Miracles 324 T

71

I have indeed misunderstood the world, because I laid my sins on it and saw them looking back at me. How deceived was I to think that what I feared was in the world, instead of in my mind.

A Course in Miracles 418 T

10 SIN

The Course says some unconventional and at times even radical things about sin. Perhaps the most difficult of these for some of us to accept is that we are not sinners, and that sin does not exist. (95T, 16: 4-6; 419 W, 5:5) On the surface, this one statement may seem to take away a major belief and underpinning of conventional Christianity. For example, if there is no original sin, then why did Jesus die? But the Course, written by the living Christ, gently corrects the idea that Jesus died for our sins. Instead, it says that he died to show us, in part, that we too are the Christ -- invulnerable and eternal.

When the Course uses the word "sin," it reframes it as being a *mistake* or an error. It says, "Let us be glad that *you will see what you believe*, and that it has been *given* you to *change what you believe*." [my italics] (652T, 6:1). In Table 20, I have summarized some of what the Course says about the origin and other characteristics of sin, in contrast to its reframe of error or mistake.

Table 20.
Some Characteristics of Error/Mistake and Sin
according to ACIM

Characteristic	Error/Mistake	Sin
Origin	We make mistakes when we are ego attached	ego makes sin, and believes we attacked God
Effect on us & God	None	Makes both God and us incomplete

Table 20 ... concluded

Characteristic	Error/Mistake	Sin
Results	Mistake corrected by Holy Spirit, who then brings peace	Guilt/shame for sinning and fear of God's punishment for it. Desire to attack others.
Description	We can be mistaken and even deceive ourself and turn our mind against ourself.	The grand illusion underlying the ego's grandiosity.
ego's insane religion	Ego sees all our mistakes as sins	Sin is real and we are "holy" to accept ourself as sinful.
Holy Spirit	Sees all our mistakes as a call for Love and correction	ego does not see or respond to Holy Spirit's Truth
Calls for	Correction	Guilt/Shame and fear of punishment
Solution	We ask Holy Spirit to correct any mistake, then surrender to It ("Let go, let God")	No solution -- only a viscous cycle of belief in sin and fear

THE "LAWS OF CHAOS"

In our mind, the idea of separation made the ego, which then made sin. The ego interpreted sin as our attack on God, for which we feel guilt and shame, since we believe that we caused sin. We also believe that we *are* sin, and for all these reasons, we then fear God, since we believe He will punish us for doing and being all of these "bad" things.

Trying to get free of it, we project our "sin" onto others, and then attack them for it. But we can't seem to get free of sin and its pain. The Course says, "You never hate your brother for his sins, but only for your own. Whatever form his sins appear to take, it but obscures the fact that you believe them to be yours, and therefore meriting a "just attack." (651T, 1:5-6).

While the Course speaks of the above sequence at different places throughout the Text and elsewhere, it is perhaps most concisely described in Chapter 23 in the section called "The Laws of Chaos" (489-494T), which I summarize in Table 21. The notion of sin is an integral part of this insane sequence of the ego's thinking process. Totally devoid of the Holy Spirit's accurate view that these chaotic "laws" do not exist, the ego, in all its grandiose thinking, bases its laws on separation and its grand illusion of sin.

THE EGO'S GRAND ILLUSION

Underlining its grandiosity, sin is the ego's grand illusion, as shown in Table 18. The ego sees sin in everyone, and uses bodies to make it possible. As the basis of its own insane religion, the ego tells us that sin is real and that we are "holy" when we believe we are sinners. Sin is thus the basis for much of our pain: our guilt, shame, fear and anger. But at the same time our "sin" is so shameful to us that we keep it hidden, a call for help we keep unheard and thus unanswered. (404T, 4:8-9)

75

1) **Separateness** - Truth is different for everyone. We each have a separate set of thoughts than others, and use them to attack others and God.

2) **Sin reinforces** - We each are sinners, who deserve attack and death by others and God. This belief reinforces separateness and fear of them.

3) **God punishes us** - God accepts our belief that we are sinners, and hates us (vengeance) for it.

4) **We punish** (attack) **others** - We believe that we own what we take from others (while in truth we take only from ourself).
Our enemy's treachery demands his death so that we can live. We attack only in self defense.

5) **ego over God** - There is a substitute for love: the ego's plan of separation which we believe is true.

Table 21.
The Laws of Chaos from ACIM [6]

The Course also addresses the relationship of sin and sickness. In our wrong mind, i.e., when we are ego attached, we conventionally believe that sin is what causes sickness and even death (e.g., from the Bible: "the wages of sin is death"). But the Course says that it is separation that causes all sickness (554T, 2) and that death does not happen, since we are eternal. The notion of sin thus joins sickness, the ego, and all of our

---

[6] The Course says that these are "laws" that we made up, but never understood and cannot find meaningful.

76

unnecessary pain as actually coming from our more primal *illusion of separation*, which the Course describes as *our only problem*.

Special relationships run on sin. (451T, 1:1) In them we project our own imagined sin onto others and then see it in them, which gives us reason to attack them. (508T, 4) The field of clinical psychology has a name for this ego defense mechanism: projective identification (described in some detail in Chapter 6 of my book *Boundaries and Relationships* (Whitfield 1993). In our special relationships what we trust is our own ego, and every person, place or thing becomes our enemy, feared and attacked, dangerous and hated. (507T, 1:1-3) But does our attachment to the idea of sin ever bring us peace? The Course poetically suggests not: "Sin is a block, set like a heavy gate, locked and without a key, across the road to peace." (475T, 3:2) It also says that it is hard for us to realize the Atonement by fighting against sin. (389T, 4:7) The Course says more about sin, some of which I summarize in Table 22 on the next page.

A WAY OUT

So, is there a way out of our attachment to our ego and its insane and painful notion of sin? The Course says that there is: "As sin is an idea you taught yourself, forgiveness must be learned by you as well, but from a Teacher other than yourself, who represents the other Self in you."(214 W, 6:3) That Teacher is God's Trinity that resides already and always within each of us.

In contrast to the ego, which sees sin as real and uncorrectable -- God's Holy Spirit doesn't see sin at all. Rather, It sees only errors or mistakes that are each a call for love and correction, as shown in Table 18. We all make mistakes when we are attached to our ego. But alone, we don't have the power to handle our mistakes as constructively as we can when we follow the Holy Spirit. As in our practice of miracles, we simply ask the Holy Spirit to help us correct any mistake we make, and then surrender to It (i.e., "Let go, and let God").

Table 22. **Some Descriptions of Sin** from ACIM

An idea you taught yourself	A perceptual error
The ego's foundation and grand illusion	An error in special form the ego venerates
Insanity, the home of all illusions	A senseless dream, a choice for death
A belief we impose between ourself and others	A block to peace
Belief we can project attack outside our mind (where the belief arose).	Belief in sin builds a world of shadows and illusions
The ego sees sin in everyone and uses bodies to make it possible	Everything God created is forever without sin
The source of our pain (guilt, shame, anger and fear)	We are not sinners. Sin does not exist
Desire to attack	No one is punished for sins
Perceiving "sin" (lack of love) we become defensive because we expect attack	To have Christ's vision is to save the world from sin
Sin is arrogant	There is no sin when we remember God

11 INNOCENCE

As I look at the numerous newborn infants I have seen over decades as a physician, father and grandfather, I am reminded that we are innocent at our core. If God made us, and we are each a part of God, how can we as newborn infants also be sinners? The Course suggests that we are not. Rather than being born in "original sin", the Course says that we are born innocent. We are already and eternally innocent.

While the Course describes various aspects of innocence, it defines it as being the same as having Christ's vision, which it also calls true perception and right mindedness (see Table 23). Innocence means that we never see what does not exist (i.e., the ego and its world), and always see what does (God and God's real world). (38T, 2:6) As shown in Table 24, at the core of our being what we are innocent or unaware *of* is our ego and its world of pain. The Course says "The innocence of God is the true state of the mind of His Son. In this state your mind knows God, for God is not symbolic; He is Fact. ...The Atonement, not sacrifice is the only appropriate gift for God's altar, where nothing except perfection belongs. The understanding of the innocent is truth. That is why their altars are truly radiant." (38T, 8:1-5)

The classic romantic poets, especially William Blake, spoke often of our innocence. In his long poem "Songs of Innocence and Experience," Blake said that we are innocent and that we can contact our innocence through the child within us (Blake 1794). In Workbook lesson 182 the Course says "... there is a Child in you who seeks his Father's house.... This childhood is eternal, with an innocence that will endure forever." (339w, 4:3-4) To me, this is one of the most moving of the 365 workbook lessons.

True Perception	Pure in heart
Right mindedness	Christ's vision
Wisdom	God Realization
Grace	Cannot project
Our true state of mind	Incapable of sacrificing anything
Eternal	Meaning of Atonement is apparent here
Joyous	Other references throught the Course

Table 23.
Some Characteristics of Innocence from ACIM

After reading the last section entitled The "Hero" of the Dream in Chapter 27 of the Text, I realized that upon entering the dream of the ego's world, we *unknowingly* caused our pain. We were and are innocent, and were simply in a dream. (585T and ff) (I discuss the dream further in Chapter I.)

Our ego	Judgment
ego's world	Punishment
Sin	Sacrifice
Evil	Death
Guilt/shame and fear	Anything else that God did not Create

Table 24.

What We Are Innocent or Unaware of ...

The author of the Course, Jesus, the living Christ, says, "...the lamb of God who taketh away the sins of the world... speaks of my innocence. The lion and the lamb lying down together symbolize that strength and innocence are not in conflict, but naturally live in peace. 'Blessed are the pure in heart for they shall see God' is another way of saying the same thing."(37T, 5:1-4) He says that a pure mind knows that innocence is strength.

The Course says that whenever we are in conflict we are in our ego, projecting sin, guilt and shame onto the person(s) with whom we are in conflict. If we see sin and badness in another we lose the peace of our innocence. If we see any error in them and attack them for it, we hurt ourselves. (41T, 7:1) It says that "You cannot know your brother when you attack him. ...You are making him a stranger by misperceiving him, and so you cannot know him." (41T, 7:4)

81

We enter into our innocence each time that we co-create a miracle. Addressing our innocence and humility, the Course says:

"Let us be still an instant, and forget all things we ever learned, all thoughts we had and every preconception that we hold of what things mean and what their purpose is. Let us remember not our own ideas of what the world is for. We do not know. Let every image held of everyone be loosened from our minds and swept away."

"Be innocent of judgment, unaware of any thoughts of evil or of good that ever crossed your mind of anything. Now do you know him not. But you are free to learn of him, and learn of him anew. Now is he born again to you, and you are born again to him, without the past that sentenced him to die, and you with him. Now is he free to live as you are free, because an ancient learning passed away and left a place for truth to be reborn." (648T, 12&13)

...their joy is in the innocence they see, and thus they seek for it because it is their purpose to behold it and rejoice.

A Course in Miracles 526T, 1:3

---

12 GRANDEUR VERSUS GRANDIOSITY

Addressing the two feeling states of grandeur and grandiosity sets the stage for a further discussion of the dynamics of joy and shame in our life. These are best described in a few pages in Chapter 9 of the Text. (p 177-180), which I recommend reading for the Course's full description. To assist in our understanding, I here summarize my take on what it says about grandeur and grandiosity. We can begin by looking at Table 25 below.

All of our grandeur is of God only. Likewise, all of our grandiosity is of our ego. Thus, our grandeur is real, while our grandiosity is an illusion, as is true of all aspects of these two worlds—God's real world and the ego's illusory one. The Course says, "Grandeur is of God, and only of Him. Therefore it is in you." (177T, 1:1-2) It may be hard for many of us, having grown up in a family and world that told us that we were bad, to realize that we are not only good, but we are great, and that in each of us is God's grandeur.

HEALING OUR SHAME

To compensate for feeling that we are so bad, i.e., so full of shame (which the Course calls *guilt*), we listen to our ego which charms us into feeling grandiose, or self-inflation - an exaggerated kind of false pride. Our ego's grandiosity is thus a *cover for our shame.* (including our guilt, "sin", and what the Course also calls littleness and despair.) So, whenever we are feeling or behaving in a *grandiose* way, which the Course describes as being *competitive, attacking* or *trying to outdo others and God*, we are usually feeling the pain of being in our ego. These others whom we are attacking or trying to outdo are what the Course calls *special relationships* (described in some detail in the Course and summarized in *Choosing God*).

83

Characteristic	Grandiosity	Grandeur
Manifestation and Result	Being competitive, attacking, trying to outdo others and God	Extending God's and our love and joy
Origin	ego	God
Truth/Reality	Unreal	Real
Function	A cover for belief in our shame [littleness, guilt, sin, despair]	Establishes our freedom and is our abundance.
Summary	A call for Love	An essential part and experience of each of us as God's Child

Table 25.

Grandiosity and Grandeur as described in ACIM

This pain of *being grandiose* in our ego *is not necessary*. It serves no useful purpose other than to remind us that we are in our ego. As we choose God, each time that we co-create a miracle, all we need to do is remember what the Course says: "Whenever you become aware of it [your *grandeur*], however dimly, you abandon the ego automatically, because in the presence of the grandeur of God the meaninglessness of the ego becomes perfectly apparent." (177T, 1:2)

WE ARE FULL OF GOD'S GRANDEUR

God's grandeur is in us, as us. Our ego is immobilized in the presence of God's grandeur because it establishes our freedom and is our abundance. We are full of God's grandeur. It then extends the love and joy that are inherently in God and in each of us. The Course says, "Your grandeur will never deceive you but your illusions always will." And what we give, we receive. It says that, "It is easy to distinguish grandeur from grandiosity, because love is returned and pride is not. Pride will not produce miracles, and will therefore deprive you of the true witnesses to your reality. ... God wants you to behold what He created because it is his joy." (179T, 7:6; 8:1-5)

When we are feeling shame, (low self-esteem, low self-worth, not good enough, etc) we can remember that the Course says that *we are altogether irreplaceable in the Mind of God*. (179t, 10:1) Rather than misinterpret our inherent God-given grandeur as somehow being arrogant, we can instead remember that accepting ourself as God created us is to deny arrogance. It says, "To accept your littleness *is* arrogant, because it means that you believe your evaluation of yourself is truer than God's," (179T, 10:9) and "...you did not establish your value and it needs no defense. Nothing can attack it or prevail over it." (180T, 11:1-2)

The Course says that our ego's grandiosity is a call for love. Whenever we or another become grandiose, it is a search for love. It says, "My birth in you is your awakening to grandeur. ... My kingdom is not of this world because it is in you. And you are of your Father." (308T, 9:5-8)

LITTLENESS AND MAGNITUDE

The Course describes grandiosity and grandeur in a similar way when it discusses littleness and magnitude (our inherent greatness in God.) In studying the Course I understand *littleness* to be the shame (which the Course calls guilt) that our ego projects onto us and others, and grandiosity to be the way our ego then tries to mask or cover up that shame. By contrast, grandeur and magnitude are a part of the spectrum of God's Love that is inherent as the Trinity within each of us.

I view the Course's description of littleness and magnitude as a continuation of that begun in its discussion of our grandeur, and summarize some of its main points in Table 26. Littleness comes from our ego and is therefore not real, and it happens when we belittle ourself. No form of it can give us peace. By contrast, *magnitude* and grandeur are from God, are real, and happen when we see our inherent glory as God's love in us. It is our peaceful home and function.

Term	Littleness	Magnitude
Origin	Ego	God
Truth	Unreal	Real
Conclusion	No form of it can bring us peace	Our peaceful home and function
Result	Belittling ourself and feeling pain	Seeing our glory as God's love in us.

Table 26. Littleness and Magnitude

HOSTAGE TO THE EGO OR HOST TO GOD?

Every decision we make answers this question. God gave Himself to us when he created us, and thereby established us as host to Him forever. In every decision we make, we choose God and Heaven, or our ego and hell. (307T, 5:1-7) We can enlist the assistance of the Holy Spirit to help us realize our inherent greatness in God, i.e., our magnitude and grandeur, and not accept the shame (i.e., our guilt, littleness and our attempts at covering them up by grandiosity) that our ego tries to dump on us. (308T, 8:7)

By practicing miracles and experiencing our grandeur, we gradually learn to stop giving or accepting littleness (shame). (308T, 5: 6-7) We discover the Christ in us, which is our awakening to our inherent grandeur that is God's love in us. (308T, 9: 5-9) We learn to do this in part by not hearing and appealing to another's appeal to hell and littleness but by hearing only his call for Heaven and greatness. (309T, 12:3) We can continue to do all of this by practicing miracles.

The ego seeks to divide and separate.

Spirit seeks to unify and heal.

A Course in Miracles 110 T

13 THE ATONEMENT

**The Atonement may be the closest term to
what sages and spiritual writers have called "enlightenment."**

Whether you prefer to pronounce it as *A-tone-ment* or *At-one-ment*,
this is a multi-dimensional and experiential manifestation of God's truth
that we can eventually learn from as we live in this world day to day.

Like miracles and forgiveness, the Atonement is unnecessary in
heaven. But in our current life we need it to heal our pain. We experience
the Atonement's multiple healing dimensions, some of which I show in
Table 27, by practicing miracles and forgiveness.

The Course says that accepting the Atonement for ourself is our only
task. To do that, we can *realize* the *unreality of sin, guilt/shame and death*
as well as *practice miracles.* This experience and process is described
throughout this book and the Course, and it comes to us each time that
we choose God. When we offer a miracle to a brother or sister, we also
offer it to ourself *and* to Jesus, the author of the Course, who is in charge
of the process of Atonement. (8T, 1:1-5)

Jesus says that his part in the Atonement is to cancel out all errors that
we can't correct, and that when we recognize our original state as God's
Child *and his brother*, we naturally become part of the Atonement. He
says that we share his unwillingness to accept error in ourself and others
and that we have the power to work miracles if we choose. Doing
miracles brings us each conviction and the ability to do more miracles.
The Course says that, "The ability is the potential, the achievement is its
expression, and the Atonement, which is the natural profession of the
children of God, is the purpose." (8t, 1:6-10) Since it is so important, I
summarize this statement on the next page.

89

OUR POTENTIAL → IS OUR ABILITY TO DO MIRACLES

Miracles → are its achievement

Miracle's purpose → is the Atonement

Table 27.
Some Characteristics of the Atonement

Perfect Love	Its message: we are guiltless
Endless and eternal	The One universal need in this world
Oneness	The way to peace
For us all	A lesson in sharing
The resurrection established it	Is in, but not for time
Only defense that we can't use destructively	Serves the miracle.

The way out of fear, guilt and shame	Radiates truth
Its means are the forgiven	Inspired by the Holy Spirit
Gentle	Our natural profession
Can only heal	The result of ego undoing and undoes all errors and the source of fear
The living Christ (Jesus) is in charge of its process	Restores our awareness of and therefore unites us with others and God
Those who accept it are invulnerable	The final lesson

THE ATONEMENT PLAN

The Atonement plan is to *release* ourself and others from the burdensome and distracting pain of the ego's *special relationships*. Practicing miracles is our way to achieve and experience that release. We realize the Atonement when we "return" to our original state as God's Child as pure spirit-mind-consciousness. (9T, 3) As such we are eternally in God's grace.

The Course says:

Spirit is in a state of grace forever.

Your reality is only spirit.

Therefore you are in a state of grace forever.

A Course in Miracles 10T, 5:4-6

The Course says that what we *see and experience inside* ourself we will project onto others. This is one of the more complex dynamics in the Course, so bear with me. Since our projection (what we give, say or do) makes our perception (what we see, hear and otherwise perceive), we then see in others what we project onto them. Then we behave with them according to *what we think we see* in them. But to see clearly and behave appropriately, we can call on and co-create miracles with God/Holy Spirit/Jesus, which then lead us to experiencing the peace and love of the Atonement.

The Course says, "The impersonal nature of miracles is because the Atonement itself is one, uniting all creatures with their Creator." As an expression of what we truly are, the miracle places our mind in a state of grace [which is part of our inherent state]. Our mind then naturally welcomes the Host [God/Holy Spirit/Jesus] within and the stranger without. "When you bring in the stranger, he becomes your brother." (10T, 6-7; 10T, 7:3-6) I understand this quote to mean that when we realize and experience our own holiness, we can more easily see the holiness in others. And, of course, vice versa: *Seeing holiness in another facilitates experiencing our own.*

Miracles thus help extend our peace and awareness of God's love to others, from which "...a strong chain of Atonement is welded." (10T, 9:1-2) By joining our mind, as our right mind, in the service of the Holy Spirit, the miracle joins in the Atonement. It does so by experientially opening us to our awareness of Love's presence and thus our Spirit within, which is eternally free.

Our ego-attached wrong mind is full of illusions and pain, while our God-conscious right mind is at peace and invulnerable. (11T, 2) A major function of the Atonement is that it restores our awareness of God's world to us. (11T, 3:6) The Course says: "Atonement corrects illusions, not truth. Therefore, it corrects what never was." (5M, 2:2-3)

A BETTER WAY

Separation is synonymous with exclusion and dissociation, and the Course says that *projection* is the *ego's main defense* to maintain the illusion of all three of these imagined states. (96T, 3:2) Projection is the main device that the ego uses to make us feel different, separated from, and "better" than others. And it is always a means of justifying attack. Yet projection will always hurt us and bring us pain.

A few months before Jesus dictated the Course to Helen and Bill, Bill had said to Helen, "There's got to be a better way" for us to get along. Helen responded positively and she agreed with him to search for that with him. Eventually it came to them as the Course, which describes that better way. While the ego projects, the Holy Spirit extends. "The Holy Spirit begins by perceiving you as perfect. Knowing this perfection is shared, He recognizes it in others, thus strengthening it in both. Instead of anger this arouses love for both, because it establishes inclusion. Perceiving equality, the Holy Spirit perceives equal needs. This invites Atonement automatically, because Atonement is the one need in this world that is universal. To perceive yourself this way is the only way in which you can find happiness in the world." (97T, 5:1-6)

The Atonement helps us experience and know that we are each a part of God's Kingdom of Oneness and Wholeness. For us to live God's will for us, which is to *co-create with Him* and have *peace and joy*, we can practice miracles and thereby gradually realize the Atonement. The Course says, "God created his Sons by extending His Thought, and retaining the extension of His Thought in His Mind. All His Thoughts are thus perfectly united within themselves and with each other. The Holy Spirit enables you to perceive this wholeness *now.* You cannot extend His Kingdom unless you know of its wholeness." (97T, 8:1-5)

14 THE HOLY INSTANT

In describing the holy instant, the Course says, "Can you imagine what it means to have no cares, no worries, no anxieties, but merely to be perfectly calm and quiet all the time?" (301T, 1:1) This is the eternal Now that sages and spiritual masters have spoken and written about in one way or another for millennia. With the help of the Holy Spirit, we can now use time to heal the pain of our special relationships and thus experience the peace of God now, which is the holy instant (sometimes capitalized as the Holy Instant).

In Chapter 14 of *Choosing God*, I showed my conception of a visual scheme of the interrelationship among some terms in the Course. I show it again here to illustrate how the holy instant relates to and flows from *miracles, true perception, forgiveness, right mind, salvation* and the *Atonement* (Figure 3). Using the term the "holy instant" is just another way of describing each of these other terms that we can use to represent the *Peace of God*.

The Course says that the condition of love is met in the holy instant, since - without the body's interference - minds are joined in peaceful communication. Throughout Chapter 15 of the text, which is entitled "The Holy Instant," the Course refers to the *body*'s influence by describing its negative aspects through a number of terms, including sin, guilt/shame, sacrifice, attack, special relationships, littleness, grandiosity, and deprivation —all of which are actually parts of the ego and its world of pain. (We can remember that The Course says that the body is *neutral*, depending on how we look at it.)

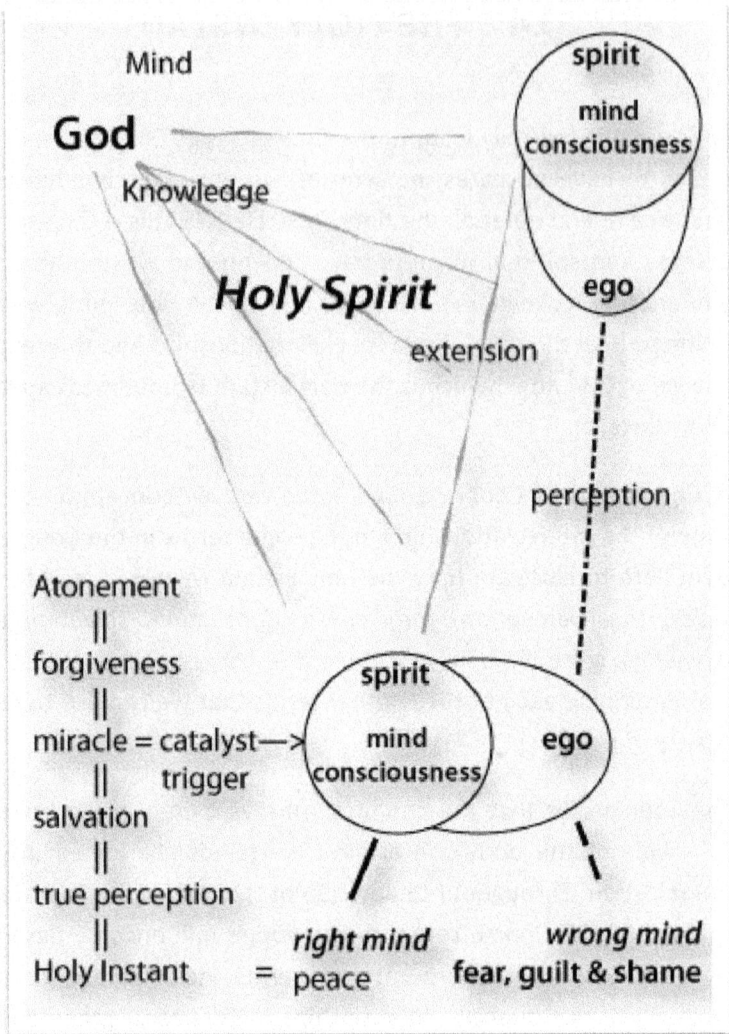

Figure 3.
A Scheme of the Interrelationship among Some Terms in ACIM

The ego believes in hell, teaches it, and holds it as its goal. It not only wants us to suffer -- it wants us dead, but not itself. (301T, 3:3) It uses time and dissociation to keep us off guard with the pain that we let it generate. By contrast, the Holy Spirit knows and teaches that there is no hell and gently uses time as the holy instant to realize the goal of a peaceful eternal life. (See also Table 2 on page 12 and 13 of Chapter 2 on Time above for other differences between the ego and the Holy Spirit.)

Practicing miracles ushers us into the experience of the peace of the holy instant. (303T, 12:4) In this way we can unchain ourselves and others by refusing to support any of our imagined "weakness." (305T, 3:6) By doing so we let go of all littleness and grandiosity, as described in the previous chapter. This is because peace is only of God, which we experience through miracles—when we are humble before God, yet still great *in* God. (310T, 3:1)

The Course says that truth is simple, while the ego tries to make our world complex. When we are experiencing God's truth, we are in our right mind, wherein we don't try to change anything, but merely accept everything. (311T, 6:7) (We can remember the Buddhist wisdom that suffering happens when we resist what is.) Since we are always safe in God's hands, we don't have to change anything or anyone. We can stay in the holy instant more easily when we remember: "...you are host to God, and hostage to no one and to nothing." (311T, 9:10)

Suspending All Judgment

In the holy instant we suspend all judgment, while we let the Holy Spirit teach us the meaning of love. Without being attached to our ego, we and everything else are already and always love. (312T, 1) The Course says that there is no substitute for love, although our ego tries to offer us weak substitutes regularly under many guises.

Mostly through our unconscious mind, the ego uses the past and future to manipulate us. In my experience, in the healing process we can bring these unconscious attempts into our conscious awareness by re-experiencing our past over the course of Stage Two recovery and accurately name what happened for us, which then helps us to eventually let our associated pain go. Then, without the pain of the past, plus knowing we are always safe in God's hands, we can let go of worrying about the future and thereby surrender into the peace of the eternal Now —the holy instant.

Safe in God's hands, we now have no intrusive personal needs. In the holy instant no one is special, and thus we have no painful special relationships. God knows us each only in His eternal Now as His perfect child, which the holy instant reflects, helping us to suspend all judgment of ourself and others (313T, 9)

> **...in the holy instant, free of the past, you see that [Gods] love is in you, and you have no need to look without and snatch love guiltily from where you thought it was.**
>
> (314T, 9:7)

Through the Atonement and in the holy instant we unite with God and all others in the Self that the Sonship shares, which is the Christ in God. (314T, 10:8-10) It is here and now that we can experience, know and understand the meaning of God's love. No other love can satisfy us, because there is no other love, being complete and asking nothing. (317T, 1:2-5) When we see with Christ's vision, we are in the holy instant, and vice versa. And with God's love in us, we have no other need but to extend it.

In the holy instant the veil of ego-attachment and time that previously "covered" God's world is lifted. Once we experience this lifting of the veil and feel God's love, without fear, we feel peace and joy. The Holy Spirit is the One that lifts the veil, which *we* initiate each time that we choose God and thereby co-create another miracle.

Table 28.

Some Characteristics of the Holy Instant as described in *ACIM*

...continued on next page

Comes from our willingness and is God's will	Is eternal, in this and every instant that we want
The experience of the peace and joy of God	Holy Spirit's most useful learning device to teach love's meaning
Frees us and our brothers [and sisters]	Will come to both in a special relationship at the request of either
Calls us each to be ourself, within its safe embrace	Where the laws of God prevail
What every situation is meant to be	Does not replace the need for learning
The time of Christ	The miracle's abiding place
Inherent within us and always available	Wherein we bring and leave all of our problems
A time of giving and receiving perfect communication	Where and when we experience the love within us

Experienced when we know we are worthy and willing	Wherein we recognize God's gift of relationships without limits
The Holy Spirit gently lays it on the ego's insanity	The shining example of every relationship and situation seen whole
A miniature of heaven and eternity	A picture of timelessness set in a frame of time
Reaches to eternity and the Mind of God	An instant of recognition shared
Loves messenger, it never fails	When we release every plan but God's
Being humble	The release from the pain of littleness and grandiosity
Purpose is to suspend judgment entirely	Where we recognize love in us, uniting it with God's mind and thus all of us
Here the veil of time and separation are lifted	Experience no bodies, only the attraction of God

In the holy instant you see in each relationship what it will be when you perceive only the present. (313T, 8:5). You are host to God, and hostage to no one and to nothing else. (311T, 9:10)

14 HOLY RELATIONSHIPS

I began an introductory description of special and holy relationships in Chapter 2 of *Choosing God*, and have continued it throughout that first book on the Course and this second one. This is because understanding these relationships is fundamental and pivotal to our ability to experience peace and joy while we are on this planet. Every concept in the Course— from our ego to our mind, from perception to the Holy Spirit—are woven into the fabric of our experience of special and holy relationships. These two ways of relating to ourself, others and God reflect our experience when we are in either of the only two worlds in which we can reside: the ego's world and God's world.

SPECIAL RELATIONSHIPS

Special relationships happen when we attach ourself to our ego. We are thereby caught and distracted in a major part of the ego's world, which we can know that we are *in* each time that we are *upset* or *in pain* —whenever we are *not at peace*.

The Course's use of the word *special* can be confusing, since we may be used to its more conventional use. Ordinarily we may use that term to refer to our meaningful relationships. For example, we may view our loved ones as being "special," since they are each unique in our experience and fill some of our healthy human needs. And in these and other ways, they *are* meaningful to us. But the Course uses the word *special* in a different way. It refers to relationships wherein *we feel* somehow *separated* or *isolated from* and *better (or worse) than* others. As a result, we are usually either in pain or ego inflated. A special relationship is thus an *ego-oriented* one, where we remain attached and listening to our ego instead of being in harmony with our real self and God. Knowing what we do about the ego, our special relationships can have many and varied characteristics, some of which I summarize in Table 27 below.

Being in special relationships is painful. They keep our awareness focused away from the Now and onto the past and future, on our bodies, false perceptions—and ultimately on our ego's painful world. They appear as two main types: special *love* and special *hate* relationships In both we project our imagined but unowned, seemingly inherent shame and guilt onto another person or others—and then blame them for our own pain. (This is also what happens, in part, in the psychological dynamic called *projective identification*, which I describe in some detail in Chapter 6 of my book *Boundaries and Relationships*.) Of the two, special *hate* relationships are the easier to understand. The special hate relationship is the more obvious of the two, since we resent or hate a person or group -- usually for some way that we think they are different from us. By contrast, in a special *love* relationship we also have a sense of love for the person mixed in with an underlying resentment. Here our love is conditional. For example, if *you* will just love me enough or in a certain way (both of which *I* determine), then I will love you back.

Table 29 shows some 24 characteristics of special relationships, and most of them are confusing and painful. Trying to find peace and love elsewhere, i.e., outside of ourself, we search and search, constructing one special relationship after another with people, places and things. In one of its most profound descriptions of addictions, the Course says, "You must have noticed an outstanding characteristic of every end that the ego has accepted as its own. When you have achieved it, *it has not satisfied you*. This is why the ego is forced to shift ceaselessly from one goal to another [including special relationships], so that you will continue to hope it can yet offer you something."(155T, 2:5-7)

102

Table 29.

Some Characteristics of Special Relationships from ACIM

...continued top of next page

Involve much pain	Do not exist in Heaven
An attempt to re-enact the past and change it (aka repetition compulsion)	A meaningless attempt to raise other gods
Exists in the past and future, and not in the present	Are meaningless without a body
The mistaken belief that separation is salvation	Inside is a conviction of littleness (guilt/shame)
Acting out vengeance on ourself	A ritual of form...at the expense of content
Excludes wholeness in relationships	The ego's answer to God's creation of the Holy Spirit
No relationship	An unhappy dream
Based on differences, where each thinks the other has what he doesn't have	Holy Spirit uses it as a learning experience that points to the truth

The rejection of God's Love	Our attraction to it fades.
Protects a delusional thought system	The opportunity to ask the Holy Spirit to release you
We seek in them what we have thrown away	The Holy Spirit transforms them into Holy Relationships
We blame our brother for our relationship's failure	Transformed, will bring freedom and joy.

Like the relationships in a soap opera, special relationships are often frustrating, and in the long run offer and usually bring us only pain. And so our attraction to them eventually fades. At that point, we may give up on most or even all of our relationships. But the Course tells us not to be discouraged.

HOLY RELATIONSHIPS

The Course says that while we may think that our special relationship's glass is half empty, that in truth our glass is actually half full. This is because a special relationship is also an *opportunity* to *ask the Holy Spirit* to *release* us from its associated *pain*. If we do so by continually asking for help through miracles—as we repeatedly choose God—and surrender to letting God's Holy Spirit help us, then It will. With our surrender, patience and persistence, the Holy Spirit will then transform our special relationship into a Holy Relationship, and we will begin to feel more peace, love and even joy.

104

Characteristics	Special	Holy
To identify which it is, we:	Are upset or in pain. and not at peace	Feel good – love, peace, &/or joy
Purpose	Destroy Reality and substitute illusion	The goal of special relationships
Basis	Separation/ego	Unity; established in Heaven
Goal	Special love/hate	Holiness; love, peace and joy
Dynamics	ego's chief defense to protect its insane thought system	Holy Spirit's gentle correction
Description	Superficial, illusory substitute for God's Will	Inherent in us and God
Experience of our truth in God	Distract us from It.	Facilitates It.
Ways to Experience	Anything from the ego's world	Faith, prayer, miracles, humility and surrender
Praises	ego in continuing hate; makes pain	God in happy song Heals pain

Table 30.

Some Differences between Special and Holy Relationships

As shown in Table 30 above, the Holy Spirit gently corrects our painful and frustrating attachment to our ego. Indeed, Holy Relationships are inherent *in us* and in God.

The Course says that each Holy Relationship heals our pain and praises God in happy song. And we experience them through faith, prayer, miracles, humility and surrender to letting the Holy Spirit do the rest, which eventually results in our experiencing peace.

Twelve Step fellowships, such as Alcoholics Anonymous and others, speak of what the Course calls special relationships in various ways. One is the trap that we get into called *resentments*. Almost by definition, when we have a resentment toward any person, place or thing, we are most likely to be enmeshed in a special relationship. Not wanting to tolerate the emotional pain of the resentment, and not knowing what to do to heal it, we often search out our drug or behavior of choice to lessen the pain. But the Course says that there is a better way.

Other Twelve Step fellowships address special relationships. AlAnon and NarAnon, which is for the friends and family of alcoholics and other drug dependent people regularly speak of detachment with love instead of resenting and trying to control the person in their life. What they are detaching from mostly is their own ego that wants to control other people, places and things.
Special relationships are similar to **co-dependence**, which others and I have defined as focusing on others to our detriment. Co-dependents Anonymous is another group that applies Twelve Step work to any relationship that focuses on another or others to our detriment (Whitfield 1993).

The Course says that whenever we may find ourself involved in a painful or conflicted relationship we can remember that, like with any pain or conflict, we have a choice. We can stay in our ego attachment and suffer, or we can choose God, and then surrender into God's love and peace.

15 USING CREATIVITY AND CO-CREATION

Among several definitions, we have described creativity as occurring when we make the ordinary into the extraordinary (Whitfield & Whitfield 2010). Addressing the terms creative, create, Creator and creation, the Course sees the ordinary for so many of us as what results when we are attached to our ego, in a kind of default mode, self-contraction and where we are often in emotional pain. By contrast, it shows us the most successful and immediate way out of that pain as the extraordinary yet entirely natural action and result when we choose God instead and thereby co-create the peace of a miracle.

The Course has numerous lines on this key lifetime dynamic dispersed throughout its three volumes (Text, Workbook for Students, Manual for Teachers and its additional content called the Supplements), of which I will give a few examples in this chapter. It says that, "Your will to create was given you by your Creator, Who was expressing the same Will in His creation. Since creative ability rests in the mind, everything you create is necessarily a matter of will. It also follows that whatever you alone make is real in your own sight, though not in the Mind of God.) (34T, 1:3-5)

But to be such a creator/co-creator we usually need a combination of six basic parts of creativity, which I show in Figure 4 as: Imagination, Inspiration, Freedom, Healthy self-care, Perspiration (the hard work of putting together the nuts and bolts of any creative process) and Humility (addressed on pages 59 and 133). The Course has cogent comments and descriptions regarding each of these six, some of which I show in Table 31. For example on the basic part of imagination, it says that our God-given creativity resides in our mind. Our mind consists of our spirit, consciousness (awareness), our choice/decision maker, and more. By now, we know that when we are in any conflict or pain we can use our mind to remember that we can choose God over the ego and thereby co-create peace for ourselves (and usually for others with we may have been in conflict). When we forget God, we are in the default mode of our ego, as shown in Figure 4, which can only make *things*, but cannot create/co-create. The Course says "Apart from [God], he [us individually as the Son] has no power to create, and what he makes is meaningless (450T, 12:4).

As I have read and re-read it, the Course says that God has already and always created the all in His Kingdom as being perfect. But then I wondered -- why is creation and co-creation a topic or issue on so many pages of the Course? My best guess is that it is because of the constant barrage that we so commonly experience from the ego's tempting us about and promising us something that we and it may deem as being "better" or more desirable. Among its many answers the Course says,

"You must have noticed an outstanding characteristic of every end that the ego has accepted as its own. When you have achieved it, it has not satisfied you. This is why the ego is forced to shift ceaselessly from one goal to another, so that you will continue to hope it can yet offer you something." (155T, 2:5-7) (Repeated for emphasis from page 102 above)

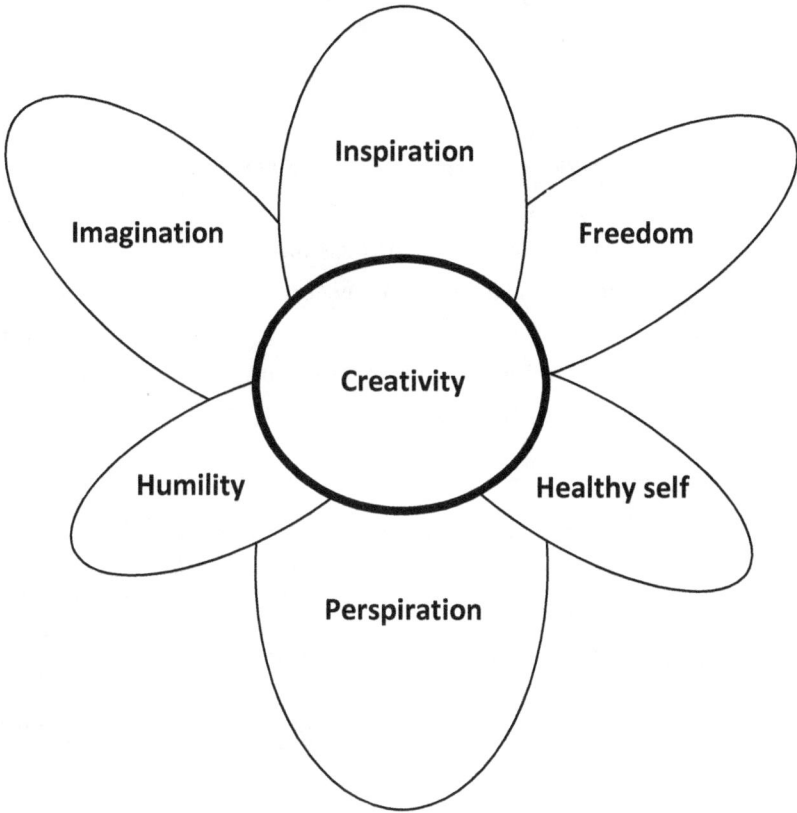

Figure 4.
The Basic Parts of Creativity – a Venn diagram

Creative Part	Example Quote(s) from the Course	Comment
Imagination	**Summary**: Our God-given creativity resides in our mind, which consists of our spirit, consciousness (awareness), choice/decision maker, and more. In any conflict or pain we can use our mind to remember [via our imagination] that we can choose God.	In 8 places the Course also sees a limited form of imagination as being more ego related (Wapnick Concordance)
Inspiration	"...you were created [by God] to create..." (112T, 3:1) "No child of God can loose this ability because it is inherent in what he is, but he can use it inappropriately by projecting." (17T, 1:1-6)	The real Muse may most often be God/Holy Spirit/Christ

Table 31.

The Basic Parts of Creativity in ACIM
as correlated from Whitfield & Whitfield 2010

Creative Part	Example Quote(s) from the Course	Comment
Freedom	"Behold the gift of freedom that I give the Holy Spirit for (you and your brother). "You are not free to give up freedom, but only to deny it." "By offering freedom you will be free."	The Course has countless references to these parts of creativity throughout its pages.
Humility	"...the essential thing is learning that *you do not know*. Knowledge is power, and all power is of God." (296T, 1:1-2)	
Self-care	***Summary***: Holy Spirit is the same loving, healing and creative Energy of God, inside of each of us which we can initiate anytime.	
Perspiration	"Trials are but lessons that you failed to learn presented once again ...In every difficulty, all distress, and each perplexity Christ calls to you and gently says, 'My brother, choose again.' " (666T, 3:1-2)	

Table 31.
The Basic Parts of Creativity
in ACIM Concluded

To further explain this seeming contradiction that God has created God's world (which includes each of us) already and always perfect, and that yet we and our world do not appear to be so, I have used the Course's sometime references to Levels and Level confusion (as often elaborated upon by Wapnick, Perry and other writers on it). As shown in Table 32, we can understand Level 1, or the "macro," as God's perfect world that he has willed to and for us, and Level 2, or the "micro," wherein God has given us His creative/co-creative and ability to choose Him/Holy Spirit/Christ over the ego.

Level	Description
1 **macro**	God wills and creates His (and our) world as already and always perfect. Also called Heaven, our awareness of God's and our perfect oneness.
2 **micro**	As a major part of God's creation, God has willed and given us His creative potential/abilities/power. And gave us both His will and our own free will so that we can choose Him or not—Him (ego/default mode/no choice). What makes us most creative is when we ask Him/Holy Spirit/ Christ as co-creator.

Table 32.
Creativity/Co-creativity according to Levels in ACIM

God's will is that we create with Him, which is co-creation. The Course says, "Child of God, you were created to create the good, the beautiful,

112

and the holy. Do not forget this." (15T, 2:1-2) We commonly create miracles when we pray to any member to the Trinity for help. To make that work, we pray with an attitude and feeling of love. It says simply,

"To create is to love. Love extends outward simply because it can not be contained. Being limitless it does not stop. It creates forever, but not in time. God's creations have always been, because He has always been. Your creations have always been, because you can create only as God creates. Eternity is yours, because He created you eternal." (112T, 3:1-9).

To Extend Love by Extension

The Course calls a main way that we love and give love by the terms extension and extend. It says, "To extend is a fundamental aspect of God which He gave to His Son [each of you and me]. In the creation God extended Himself and His creations and imbued them with the same loving Will to create. You have not only fully created, but have also been created perfect. There is no emptiness in you. Because of your likeness to your Creator you are creative. No child of God can lose this ability because it is inherent in what he is, but he can use it inappropriately by projecting." (17T, 1:1-6)

Each time that we choose God we are extending our love through the Holy Spirit which further extends love and compassion to Creation, as shown in Table 33 on the next page.

Action Category	Action Content [7]	Result: The Miracle
Thought +	Ask God for help	Holy Spirit extends to self & Creation, reverberates in Heaven, & back to self...
Feeling +	Love and Compassion	leading to *more* peace & love [8]
Attitude	Surrender to "Let go, let God"	Acceptance of other(s), leading to continued peace

Table 33.
Miracles Extend God's Healing Unconditional Love

---

[7] Our will in action.

[8] God's Will in action. (These two Wills are in such harmony that when we experience them, we will know they are the same.)

Epilogue

The Course has more topics and areas from which we can learn and grow psychologically and spiritually. In these two volumes I have summarized some 30 of them in what I saw as being its basic and main map and messages that help us answer our perennial questions of –

Who am I?

What am I doing here?

Where am I going? and

How can I get any peace?

As you begin or continue to read the Course on your own or perhaps sometimes with others, you will likely find more such topics and issues that may apply to your life. The Course's language and content are so rich and profound from both an intellectual and a psycho-spiritual perspective that you will likely see that what I have written in these two volumes is but an introduction and overview reflecting its richness and depth.

THE HEALING OF THE DREAM

In these two books I have gone from the Course's basics of who we are -- a Child of God -- to the seemingly more complex description of special and holy relationships to the ladder of prayer to the overview map/diagram on Figure 3 (page 100) to the stages and process of forgiveness. One area of our human psychological and spiritual dynamic that I have not yet addressed is that of *humor* in our lives. The course mentions it some 43 times and refers to it only through its spiritual psychology using the words Laugh, Laughs, Laughed and Laughter -- as it describes yet another aspect of the bind that we have put ourselves in when we attach to our ego instead of God. The Course says that we so buy into the ego's dream which says that we are a body in the ego's world, and that we are victims of other bodies.

Still wrapped in the dream we believe that we are separate from others and God and that we are bad (born and somehow maintained as a sinner) and thereby deserving punishment by others and God. To help fill our emptiness we substitute often dysfunctional people, places and things for our only healthy relationship which is with God and God's kingdom -- of which we and our loved ones and others are a key part. The Course says this more eloquently in a long section in Chapter 27 entitled The Healing of the Dream, "The body's serial adventures, from the time of birth to dying are the theme of every dream the world has ever had. The 'hero' of this dream will never change, nor will its purpose. Though the dream itself takes many forms, and seems to show a great variety of places and events wherein its 'hero' finds itself, the dream has but one purpose, taught in many ways. ... that it is cause and not effect. And you are its effect, and cannot be its cause." [when in fact you are] (586T, 3:1-5)

We can here return to Figure 1 in Chapter 1 on page 2 that shows us the clear *differentiation* of the ego's dream of its painful world that we bought into by attaching to it (believing it and living it as though it were real), *from* when we awaken into God's Real World. We do this by the simple message of the Course that I have summarized throughout these two books: Whenever we are in pain or we are not at peace, we can choose God, and the peace of the miracle will likely occur. But so often we still may not get it.

So the Course continues, "Thus you [*think* that you] are not the dreamer, but the dream. And so you wander idly in and out of places and events that it contrives. That this is all the body does is true, for it is but a figure in a dream. But who reacts to figures in a dream unless he sees them as if they were real? The instant that he sees them as they are they have no more effects on him, because he understands he gave them their effects by causing them and making them seem real."

It goes on, "How willing are you to escape effects of all the dreams the world has ever had? ... No one asleep and dreaming in the world remembers his attack upon himself. ... He would have seen at once that these ideas are one illusion, too ridiculous for anything but to be laughed away.

... We can remember this, if we but look directly at their cause [our ego attachment]. And we will see the ground for laughter, not a cause for fear.

In one of its oft quoted adages it says, "Let us return the dream he [i.e., us] gave away onto the dreamer, who perceives the dream as separate from himself and done to him. Into eternity, where all is one, there crept a tiny, mad idea, at which the Son of God remembered not to laugh. In his [our] forgetting did the thought become a serious idea, and possible of both accomplishment and real effects. Together, we can laugh them both away.

What we are laughing away includes what the Course continues: "A timelessness in which time is made real; a part of God that can attach itself [to our unreal ego]; a separate brother as an enemy; a mind within a body -- all are forms of circularity whose ending starts at its beginning, ending at its cause, the world you see depicts exactly what you thought you did. Except that now you think that what you did is now being done to you..."

It concludes this section: "The secret of salvation is but this: that *you are doing this unto yourself* [my italics]. No matter what the form of the attack, this still is true. ... This single lesson learned will set you free from suffering, whatever form it takes... And you will understand that miracles reflect the simple statement, ' *I* have done this thing, and it is this I would undo.' " (586T, 4-10)

117

But God has already and always handled it for us. From Chapter 1 above, I said: we can remember that the undoing of the ego, and the Atonement itself, have already been accomplished. This is because at the same instant that we thought we separated from God, God created the Holy Spirit, and thereby extended Himself directly into our illusory script-dream.

*   *   *

Going beyond commenting on the Course's 43 quotes on laugh, laughs, laughed and laughter as being humorous, I will leave you with perhaps your own possible experience of the healing power of laughter.

Study this drawing when you have the time and space to just be...

For your consideration this is a creative rendition of what could have been a prediction of what has developed over the last two thousand years as the Last Supper food fight, which, among many things, may once again represent our attachment to our ego.

119

Ideas leave not their source. Change your mind about yourself and healing will follow.

A Course in Miracles 311T

In keeping with ecumenical thinking in the process of healing, in the Appendix that follows I describe some similarities among other religions and spiritual paths, Twelve Step fellowships and the Course in **The Universal Message of the Course.**

APPENDIX

THE UNIVERSAL MESSAGE OF THE COURSE:

Other Faiths, Twelve Step Fellowships and ACIM

All of the world religions speak of the importance of our relationship with ourself, others and God. While each faith does so in its own way, their essential messages are more alike than not. The Course says that there are many paths to or interpretations of God's Holy Spirit's one universal curriculum: that we are all One and have never left God.

I have been impressed with how similar these many and seemingly diverse paths are. As two examples, I show how the **four Noble Truths of Buddhism** and the **Twelve Steps of A.A.** (shown below) are essentially the same, and which the **Course** also exemplifies in great detail.

These boil down to four main observations and principles:
1) Our human **life** has a **painful** side,
2) **Attachment to** our **ego** and anything in the ego's world **causes** our pain,
3) **Detaching** from these **lessens** our pain, and
4) To detach we can **follow a spiritual path** that includes healthy inner and outer functioning.

THE TWELVE STEPS OF ALCOHOLICS ANONYMOUS

1. We admitted we were **powerless** over alcohol -- that our lives had become **unmanageable**.

2. **Came to believe** that a **Power** greater than ourselves **could restore** us to **sanity**.

3. Made a **decision** to **turn our will** and our **lives over** to the **care of God** as we understood Him.

4. Made a **searching** and **fearless moral inventory of ourselves**.

5. **Admitted to God**, to **ourselves** and to **another human being** the exact nature of our wrongs.

6. Were **entirely ready** to **have God remove** all these **defects** of character.

7. **Humbly asked** Him to **remove** our shortcomings.

8. Made a **list of all persons we had harmed**, and **became willing** to **make amends** to them all.

9. **Made direct amends** to such people **wherever possible**, except when to do so would injure them or others.

10. **Continued** to take **personal inventory**, and when we were wrong **promptly admitted** it.

11. **Sought through prayer** and **meditation** to **improve** our **conscious contact** with God, as we understood Him, **praying** only **for knowledge of His will for us** and the **power to carry that   out**.

12. Having had a **spiritual awakening** as the result of these steps, we **tried to carry** this **message** to alcoholics, and to **practice** these **principles** in **all our affairs**. [my bold]

Given these four principles, it is often puzzling to me how many world religions and their denominations can then take them and try to use them not only against one another, but in some ways even against their own members and followers. To this dilemma Twelve Step Fellowships remain wisely detached. For example, the Tenth Tradition of AA's Twelve Traditions says, "No AA group or member should ever, in such a way as to implicate AA, express any opinion on outside controversial issues— particularly those of politics, alcohol reform, or sectarian religion. The Alcoholics Anonymous groups oppose no one. Concerning such matters they can express no views whatever." (AA 3rd edition, 1976).

Likewise, the Course says that it is but one of thousands of paths, all with the same outcome, i.e., self and God realization. It says that since God's will is unchangeable and inevitable, we will each accomplish this outcome in our own way and our own time. (e.g., 3M, 4:6) The Course offers us the advantage of *lessening* the amount of time that it may otherwise take us to reach the experience of our true self and God.

As we have evolved as a species we have had a number of religions and spiritual paths from which to choose. I show some of these below in a simple timeline. The dates when some of these are said to have begun are approximate and conservative. For example, Hinduism may have actually started farther back in time than I show here, and Judaism may have evolved from as far back as somewhere between 2,000 and 3,000 BCE (before the "common era," or BC).

EXPANSION

While it was always evolving, I believe that our understanding of spirituality began to expand more rapidly in the early part of the 20th century. Following the trend begun around 1850 in the New Thought movement in the West and the Baha'i faith in the East, with each of these rooted in the Judeo-Christian—Muslim—Buddhist—Taoist—Hindu past, an expanded and Christian – influenced spirituality was born around

1935. It was in this year that AA was founded, and four years later in April of 1939 that its "Big Book" *Alcoholics Anonymous* was published.

Figure 5.
TimeLine of world "Brand Name" religions and paths

3,000 BCE →	1,800	550 to 500	25-30 CE
Hinduism	Judaism	Buddhism	Christianity
	Taoism		
	Confucianism		

600	1850	1935	1975/6
Islam	New Thought	A.A.	ACIM
	Baha'i		

At about the same time, coincidentally or perhaps synchronistically, *The Urantia* (Earth) *Book* was completed, and some 20 years later it was published in 1955.

About a decade after that another important spiritual book was published: *A Course in Miracles* (1975-6). Each of these three modern holy books reflected a practical and experiential spirituality, often called the *esoteric* or hidden way to realizing self, others and God (as opposed to the conventional or *exoteric* religion). Actually, all prior religions also had such an esoteric component, but most of them kept it hidden, with only a small minority of their clergy and members studying and practicing it. No matter how we may look at them, these paths reflected an expansion of most conventional or mainstream religion. Twelve Step fellowships tend to be more esoteric (mystical, spiritual) than conventional.

A SPIRITUAL FORCE

I and others believe that AA and the now more than 100 other Twelve Step fellowships constitute a growing religious and spiritual force in the world. Likewise, the Course has an increasing number of students. For various reasons, some previously conventionally religious people are supplementing their primary religion with one or both of these two spiritual paths. Some are also leaving their prior religion completely, although some of them eventually return to it with a new outlook after having found a nourishing spirituality outside of it.

In addition, there is a growing number of Twelve Step fellowship members who are supplementing their spirituality with the expanded teachings of the Course. One of them said, "After 11 years in the program, making good progress, I found that I was dry or sober, but I still often felt empty. I had even tried returning to my church, but that helped me only a little. I had heard about the Course, but had not studied it or even bought a copy. Then one day a friend lent me his copy, and I began to read it. I eventually joined a Course discussion group, and started to understand what it was saying. You know, it's really just like this (holding up 2 fingers from each hand side by side) with AA. The Course has brought the Twelve Steps to life even more for me."

DEEPENING SIMILARITIES

After having studied the Twelve Steps and several of their programs for nearly 40 years and the Course for over 30 years, I noticed many of their similarities. The first is that the Course is *entirely* compatible with the Steps themselves. Not only is the Course's message in harmony with *each* of the Steps, where appropriate it also expands that Step itself. I show some examples of how I see these similarities in Table A 1.

Table A 1. Similarity of the Twelve Step with Selected Terms from Twelve Step Work and the Course.

Alcoholics Anonymous	A Course in Miracles
Step 2. Sanity	Right mindedness, seeing with Christ's vision
3. Decision (made a...)	Decision maker, choice maker
4. Moral inventory	ego undoing, forgiveness process
5, 6 & 7. Our wrongs, character defects, shortcomings	ego attachment, wrong mind, mistakes
7. Humbly asked (humility)	Humility, openness, Willingness
8 & 9. Making amends	Let go of ego / forgive
10. Continuing to take personal inventory	Vigilance for ego
11. Prayer & meditation	Prayer → miracles
Serenity	Inner peace

The Course also uses specific *terms* in a way that compliments and often provides more depth to some of the key terms from the Twelve Steps. I show some examples of these comparisons in Table A 2.

SANITY

AA refers to sanity and insanity on two levels. The first relates to the alcoholics insane thinking that he can drink normally, without experiencing detrimental effects. Thus, sanity is remembering that he cannot safely drink or use other psychoactive drugs. Insanity is forgetting that fact.

AA's second level of understanding these two terms broadens them to the mental and emotional realm of relationships with others. In Chapter 6 of AA's "Big Book" (Alcoholics Anonymous) entitled "Into Action," it says, "And we have ceased fighting anything or anyone—even alcohol. (This idea parallels the Course's statement that, "In my defenselessness my safety lies.") For by this time sanity will have returned." (AA p.84, 1976)

But how exactly does the recovering person become sane? The second Step begins to tell us how: by coming to believe that a Power greater than ourselves could restore us to sanity. The Third Step follows with the next effective action: deciding to turn our will and our lives over to the *care* of God.

Table A 2. Similarity of Selected Terms from the Twelve Steps with Some Terms in the Course

Twelve Step Work Terms	Similarity to ACIM Terms
Sanity **– Remember can't safely drink** **-- or other behavior.** ... **Insanity** -- forgetting that fact. ... Ceased fighting anything or anyone, even alcohol, others	**Sanity** defined as right mindedness, or seeing self, others and God with Christ's vision, which is true perception. **Insanity** is ego attachment, a major part of which is false perception
Let go and let God	Whenever in pain, let go ego and **choose God**.
Decision Making – several key ones e.g., "Made a decision..." (see text)	(Right) **Mind as** decision and choice maker = the real altar to God = true perception = Seeing with Christ's vision
Moral Inventory – can also see as core issues; assisted by differentiating true and false self (ego)	Reframes our wrongs or "sins" as being simply mistakes. Differentiates right v. wrong mind that chooses God v. ego as main inventory to take regularly. Course as ego guises teacher.
Humility -- foundation principle of each of the Twelve Steps	Addresses humility throughout Course. See Chapter 4 of Choosing God.

Similarity of Selected Terms from the Twelve Steps with Some Terms in the Course

Twelve Step Work Terms	*Similarity to ACIM Terms*
Making Amends – in Steps 4, 8 & 9	Make amends by process of letting go of our ego, which it also calls forgiveness.
Continuing Personal Inventory and when wrong promptly admitting it	Expanded in the Course's focus on being vigilant for our ego, and especially for God and God's kingdom.
Prayer and Meditation – Step 11, the longest of the Twelve	Prayer as a main way to co-create miracles and their resulting peace
Serenity – "…we will know peace" (Chapter 6 Big Book)	God's peace is what we feel and experience when we initiate and co-create a miracle.

The Course's teaching on these terms compliments and expands that of AA by defining sanity as right mindedness, or seeing self, others and God with Christ's vision, which it also calls true perception. Insanity is ego attachment, a major part of which is false perception, which I describe in Chapter 15. Whenever we are in pain, the Course suggests that the way to maintain our inherent and natural sanity is to go within and choose God.

Decision Making

AA's Big Book refers to the word "decision" in several ways. Perhaps its two most important include that used in Step Three: "Made a decision to turn our will and our lives over to the care of God as we understood Him," and that we need to go further by taking action that addresses what was blocking our self and God-realization. (AA p. 64, 1976) The rest of the Steps tell us how to do that.

The Course gives us an extension of AA's decision action by naming and describing our decision- or choice-maker. It says that this key and powerful part of us is inherent in us as an aspect of our mind, which I discuss in Chapter 13. It even says that our decision-maker is the *real altar* to God, and it tells us exactly how to activate and use it.

Moral Inventory

In "making a fearless moral inventory of ourselves," AA's Fourth Step continues the process of unblocking our true knowledge of self, others and God. The Steps suggest that what we need to find is what is wrong, and to some extent, what is right about ourself. In the Fifth through the Seventh Steps it calls these our "character defects," "shortcomings" or "wrongs."

From my work assisting alcoholics and other chemical dependent people and their adult children—as they recover, I have come to call these "defects" instead *core recovery issues*, or simply core issues. Here the Course has assisted me as it reframes our wrongs or "sins" as being simply mistakes. Our only problem, it says, is our illusion that we are separate from others and God, and are completely on our own. It calls this illusion our ego, and says that when we become attached to that insane part of us, we are in our wrong mind, seeing the world with false perception. The way out, it suggests, is by the process of ego undoing, letting go, or detaching. But I have noticed that to let something go with which we are so strongly identified—such as our ego—we first have to know, both mentally and experientially, *just what it is that we are letting go of*. And so the Course spends a large part of its volume describing the many guises of the ego and its insane and painful world. At the same time, it reminds us over and over that the way to let go of our ego is by choosing God over it, which is how we co-create miracles.

HUMILITY

AA's "Big Book" emphasizes the usefulness of humility about 30 times in its text. This crucial part of recovery and healing is basic to both AA and the Course's teachings. Indeed, humility is the "foundation principle" of each one of the Twelve Steps. (Twelve and Twelve 1952) One of my favorite lines from AA's *Twelve Steps and Twelve Traditions* is, "humility and intellect are compatible, provided we place humility first." (I describe an overview of how important humility is in the Course in Chapter 4 of *Choosing God* and parts of *Teachers of God*, and Wapnick does also at greater length. [Wapnick—message 1998])

MAKING AMENDS

To make amends to those we have harmed, AA says that we have begun to look within by previously having made our moral inventory. Continuing in Steps Eight and Nine, we then go within again and identify and then humbly apologize to those we have harmed. (Twelve and Twelve 1952) In these Steps we are continuing to use our spirituality to help us heal. In fact, AA says that, "Our real purpose is to fit ourselves to be of maximum service to God and the people about us." (AA, p.77, 1976)

The Course continues that purpose by its detailed description of the process of letting go of our ego, which it also calls forgiveness. As a result, we transform our painful special relationships, which are usually fraught with resentments, into holy relationships (which I describe in Chapter 14 above in more detail).

CONTINUING PERSONAL INVENTORY

AA's idea of continuing to take our personal inventory, and when we were wrong promptly admitting it, is extended and expanded in the Course's focus on being vigilant. While the Course teaches us to be vigilant for our ego, much of its efforts in this regard involve instead being vigilant only for God and God's kingdom. This emphasis keeps us focused on God's spiritual nourishment of each of us.

PRAYER AND MEDITATION

In its powerful Eleventh Step, AA suggests that we connect with God through praying and meditating. I have found nearly 25 references in the Big Book where it mentions the advantages of prayer and/or meditation. The Course focuses mostly on prayer, since that is the way that we initiate our co-creation of miracles. Indeed, it even has a supplementary booklet concentrating on it called *The Song of Prayer*. (I discuss this and the Course's teachings about prayer in Chapter 4 of *Teachers of God*.)

SERENITY

In Chapter 6 "Into Action," AA speaks of serenity as being about the same as feeling peace: "We are going to know a new freedom and a new happiness. We will not regret the past nor wish to shut the door on it. We will comprehend the word serenity and we will know peace." (AA, p 83, 1976) AA began to use "The Serenity Prayer" in 1942, commenting that "Never had we seen so much AA in so few words."

The Course's basic term for serenity is peace, or the peace of God, which I discuss in Chapters 6 and 10. of Choosing God and in several places in this book. God's peace is what we feel and experience when we initiate and co-create a miracle.

THE FOUNDERS OF ALCOHOLICS ANONYMOUS,
DR. BOB AND BILL W.

THE "FOUNDERS" OF A COURSE IN MIRACLES, KEN WAPNICK,
PHD, BILL THETFORD, PHD, HELEN SCHUCMAN, PHD,
AND JUDY SKUTCH WHITSON

References

Anonymous: *A Course in Miracles*. Foundation for Inner Peace/ Viking Penguin, 1975, 1996

Anonymous: *The Song of Prayer:* Prayer, forgiveness, healing. Foundation for Inner Peace, Box 598, Mill Valley CA 94942, 1978

Anonymous: Psychotherapy: Purpose, Process and Practice. (Booklet). Foundation for Inner Peace, Tiburon, Ca. 1976

Benor DJ: Survey of spiritual healing research. *Complementary Medical Research* 4(3): 9-33, 1990

Berke D: *Love Always Answers:* Walking the path of miracles. Crossroad, NY, 1994

Blake W: Songs of Innocence and of Experience: showing the two contrary states of the human soul, London, 1794, Rare Books and Special Collections, Princeton University Library

Byrd RC: Positive therapeutic effects of intercessory prayer in a coronary care unit Population. *Southern Medical Journal* 81 (7): 826-9, 1988

Deikman A: *The Observing Self*. Beacon Press, Boston, 1982

Dossey L: *Healing Words: The power of prayer and the practice of medicine.* Harper, San Francisco, 1993

Findisen B: *ACIM Concordance* to Volume One: Text. Coleman Graphics, Farmingdale, NY, 1983

Foundation for Inner Peace: *Concordance* of A Course in Miracles, Mill Valley, Ca 1997

Foundation for Inner Peace: Memories of Helen & Bill (DVD), Mill Valley, Ca 2010

Lazaris: Releasing negative ego. Video and audiotape Concept Synergy, Palm Beach, FL 1980, 1986

Metzger BM, Coogan MD (eds): *The Oxford Companion to the Bible*. Oxford University Press, NY, 1993

Mundy J: *Awaken to Your Own Call:* Exploring ACIM. Crossroad, NY, l994

Mundy J: *Time, Death and A Course in Miracles*. Prints of Peace, Monroe, NY,1975

Perry R: *Reality & Illusion*: An overview of Course metaphysics. Part 1. The Circle of Atonement Sedona, Az , 1993

Skutch R: *Journey Without Distance:* The story behind *A Course in Miracles*. Celestial Arts. Berkeley, Ca 1984

Sylvest VM: *The Formula* Sunstar Publishing Ltd. Fairfield, Iowa l996

Vaughan F, Walsh R: *Accept This Gift* Tarcher/Perigee Books. New York, NY 1983

Wapnick G: quoted in Davies TL: Interview with Kenneth and Gloria Wapnick. *Love and Forgiveness* 1:2 (March/April), p.23, l997

Wapnick K: *Glossary Index for ACIM*. 3rd ed. Foundation for *ACIM,* Roscoe N.Y, 1989

Wapnick K: *The Message of* A Course in Miracles. *Volume One* - All Are Called, & *Volume Two* – Few choose to listen. Foundation for *A Course in Miracles*, Roscoe, NY,1997

Wapnick K: *The Fifty Miracle Principles* of "A Course in Miracles": A Commentary on the Text, pages 1-4. Foundation for ACIM, Box 71, RR2, Roscoe, NY 12776-9506, 1985

Wapnick K: *Absence from Felicity*: The Story of Helen Schucman and Her Scribing of A Course in Miracles. Foundation for ACIM, Roscoe, NY, 1991

Wapnick K: *A Vast Illusion*: Time according to ACIM. Foundation for ACIM, Roscoe, NY, 1990

Wapnick K: Christian Psychology in ACIM (booklet). Foundation for Inner Peace, Tiburon, Ca. 1976

Wapnick, K: *The Message of A Course in Miracles. vols. 1 &2.* Foundation for *ACIM,* Roscoe N.Y, 1997

Wapnick K: Talks on ACIM. Silver Spring, MD about 1982, and Psychiatric Institute of Washington continuing education workshop about 1988

Watson A: *Seeing the Bible Differently.* The Circle of Atonement , Sedona, Az , 1997

Whitfield, BH: *Spiritual Awakenings.* Health Communications Inc, Deerfield Bch Fl 1995

Whitfield, B: *Final Passage: Sharing the Journey as This Life Ends.* Health Communications, Inc. Deerfield Bch, Florida. 1998

Whitfield, CL: Chapter 65. Co-dependence, addictions, and related disorders. in Lowinson, et al (eds): *Substance Abuse*: A Comprehensive Textbook. third edition, Williams & Wilkins, Baltimore, 1997 (also in Second Edition, 1992)

Whitfield CL: *Healing the Child Within*. Health Communications Inc, Deerfield Bch, Fl 1986

Whitfield CL: *A Gift to Myself*. Health Communications Inc, Deerfield Bch Fl 1990

Whitfield CL: *Boundaries and Relationships*. Health Communications Inc, Deerfield Bch, Fl 1993

Whitfield CL, Whitfield B: Engaging the Muse: Creativity in Relationships and Life. Muse House Press, Atlanta 2010

Williamson M: A *Return to Love*: Reflections on the principles of *A Course in Miracles.* HarperPerennial, 1993

WEBSITES FOR MORE INFORMATION ON THE COURSE:

circleofa.org. Circle Of Atonement ... honors the breadth and depth of the Course including radical, mind-expanding ideas as well as detailed instructions for practical application. ... grounded in long and close study of the Course and tested in personal experience.

www.facim.org Ken and Gloria Wapnick's informative website that presents the purpose and activities of the Foundation as well as what *A Course in Miracles*

www.acim.org website of the Foundation for Inner Peace, the original organization appointed by the scribe, Helen Schucman, to publish and distribute the only authorized manuscript of *A Course in Miracles*. *www.miraclesinactionpress.com/readers.htm*

www.miraclesinactionpress.com/links.htm.

web.archive.org/web/20060128092110/www.miraclestudies.net/Biogr aphical.html

www.facim.org/acim/glossary.htm -- Glossary on key Course terms from Ken Wapnick's website

ABOUT THE AUTHOR

Charles L. Whitfield, MD, is a pioneer in addictions and in trauma recovery, including the way we remember childhood and other trauma and abuse. A physician and frontline therapist who assists trauma survivors in their healing, he is the author of over sixty published articles and ten books, several of which are best sellers. He writes on trauma psychology, spirituality and recovery. *Healing the Child Within* and *Boundaries and Relationships* are classics in the field. Five of his books have been translated and published in eleven foreign languages.

Dr. Whitfield was one of the first physicians to teach about spirituality in recovery in a medical school setting. Since 1995 he has been voted by his peers as being one of the best doctors in America. For over twenty-three years he has taught at Rutgers University's Institute on Alcohol and Drug Studies. He recently was awarded their annual Lifetime Achievement Award by the Atlanta Therapeutic Professional Community.

He is a consultant and research collaborator at the Centers for Disease Control and Prevention since 1998 examining the aftereffects for adults that were repeatedly traumatized as children. He is a Fellow of The American Society for Addiction Medicine.

He has a private practice in Atlanta, Georgia, with his wife, Barbara, where they provide individual and group therapy for trauma survivors and people with addictions and other problems in living. He and Barbara have taught classes on *A Course in Miracles* and recently joined the faculty of the Center for Sacred Studies where they teach a module on Unity in Practice to graduating two year students becoming ordained as Ministers of Prayer. Together they serve as consulting editors for *The Journal of Near-Death Studies* and sit on the advisory board for The American Center for the Integration of Spiritually Transformational Experiences (ACISTE). For more information go to *www.barbarawhitfield.com* and *www.cbwhit.com*

INDEX

144

U

V

W

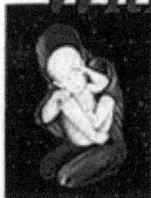

148

149

150

151

152

STRESS MANAGEMENT and SERENITY DURING RECOVERY

ALCOHOLISM

OTHER DRUG PROBLEMS **&**

& other attachments SPIRITUALITY

CHARLES L. WHITFIELD, M.D.

A TRANSPERSONAL APPROACH

Classic, Self-published, 1985.

150 pages and 437 references on general and advanced spirituality that I wrote for my students at Rutgers University Advanced School of Alcohol and Drug Studies.

I have a few extra copies left from that printing available for $18.00 including postage.

Send money order (preferred) or a good check to:
Charles Whitfield
3462 Hallcrest Drive, NE
Atlanta, GA 30319

New books by author since first printing

Whitfield CL (2012) *Not Crazy*: You May Not be Mentally Ill. Muse House Press, Atlanta, Ga

Whitfield CL (2012) *Wisdom to Know the Difference*: Core Issues in Relationships, Recovery and Living. Muse House Press

Whitfield CL, Whitfield BH (2013) *Timeless Troubadours*: The Moody Blues Music and Message. Foreword by MB's co-founder, keyboardist, composer and vocalist Mike Pinder. Muse House Press

www.ingramcontent.com/pod-product-compliance
Lightning Source LLC
Chambersburg PA
CBHW030109300326
41934CB00033B/350